"If you've ever thought of taking the entrepreneurial plunge, make *Fired Up!* your business partner. It could mean the difference between sinking and swimming." —KEN BLANCHARD, co-author of *The One-Minute Manager*

"*Fired Up!* captures the essence of American free enterprise. It pulls together the right blend of ingenuity, courage, drive, and practicality that leads to success in a new, small enterprise or a large one seeking to shake off the shackles of conformity and debilitating caution. It demonstrates why the successful entrepreneur has much in common with the creative artist. I hope that the next generation will be captured by its zest and energy."
—DAVID L. BOREN, former United States Senator
and President, The University of Oklahoma

"Thinking of going out on your own? Read this book first. It will tell you if you've got the 'right stuff' to be an entrepreneur and how to get started."
—O. BURTCH DRAKE, President and Chief Executive Officer
of the American Association of Advertising Agencies

"The highest compliment I can give this book is that I hope none of my best people at Nabisco will read it for fear that they might strike out on their own. On a more positive note, it reminded me of the critical need to nurture an environment at Nabisco where true entrepreneurial types can thrive."
—H. JOHN GREENIAUS, Chairman and Chief Executive Officer of Nabisco

"*Fired Up!* is filled with sound, practical advice for anyone planning to embark on a personal business venture. A must-read guide for the budding entrepreneur!"
—BILL HOLEKAMP, Executive Vice President, Enterprise Rent-A-Car

"This is a book that will give you a real understanding of what it takes to be a successful entrepreneur."
—ROBERT IBSEN, founder and developer of DenMat,
manufacturer of Rembrandt, the number one whitening toothpaste

"*Fired Up!* is the book you should read if you dream of building a big and successful entrepreneurial company. It really tells the truth about how to avoid many business start-up mistakes . . . and it's a fast, great read!"
—ALLAN KURTZMAN, former President of Neutrogena and Max Factor

"Michael Gill and Sheila Paterson have written a tough-minded handbook for would-be entrepreneurs, alerting them to the risks they take as well as the potential payoffs. It is also a how-to guide to making it as an entrepreneur, detailing business practices and techniques of success. Most Americans daydream about starting a business; this book provides a useful road map on how to start turning those dreams into reality. Here's hoping it leads to more entrepreneurship."

—SENATOR JOSEPH I. LIEBERMAN, Connecticut

"I wish I had read this book before I started my own business."

—FAITH POPCORN, author of *The Popcorn Report* and *Clicking*

"I'm wild about *Fired Up!* It has real application for HR professionals who are trying to create in their own organizations an entrepreneurial culture, which is the only way corporations are going to succeed ... to release the power of the individual and get everyone to behave as an entrepreneur."

—KEN RANFTLE, Senior Professional in Human Resources,
former Chairman of the Society of Human Resource Management

"Michael Gill and Sheila Paterson have produced a book which captures the spirit of entrepreneurship. It should serve as a source of inspiration for anyone seeking to start their own business venture or other entrepreneurial effort."

—FRED SMITH, founder and Chief Executive Officer, Federal Express

"Congratulations on your great book. It proves out my statement—there is a big difference between signing the *back* of the check and the *front* of the check."

—BOB TASCA, Chairman, Tasca Automotive Group; author of *You Will Be Satisfied*

"This short book provides timely advice for the many people who through volition or through necessity are starting their own business. Based on interviews with over 300 people who have made the transition from corporate life to successful entrepreneurship, the authors have written an inspirational account of the entrepreneurial world laden with practical do's and don'ts for those who venture down this path."

—VICTOR H. VROOM, John G. Searle Professor of
Organization and Management, Yale University

FIRED UP!

From Corporate Kiss-Off
To Entrepreneurial Kick-Off

Take Charge Of Your Destiny In Our Downsizing World

MICHAEL GILL
and SHEILA PATERSON

VIKING

VIKING
Published by the Penguin Group
Penguin Books USA Inc., 375 Hudson Street,
New York, New York 10014, U.S.A.
Penguin Books Ltd, 27 Wrights Lane, London W8 5TZ, England
Penguin Books Australia Ltd, Ringwood, Victoria, Australia
Penguin Books Canada Ltd, 10 Alcorn Avenue,
Toronto, Ontario, Canada M4V 3B2
Penguin Books (N.Z.) Ltd, 182–190 Wairau Road,
Auckland 10, New Zealand

Penguin Books, Ltd, Registered Offices:
Harmondsworth, Middlesex, England

First published in 1996 by Viking Penguin,
a division of Penguin Books USA Inc.

1 3 5 7 9 10 8 6 4 2

The individual experiences recounted in this book are true. However,
in some instances, names and descriptive details have been altered
to protect the identities of the people involved.

Publisher's Note
This publication is designed to provide accurate and authoritative
information in regard to the subject matter covered. It is sold with the
understanding that the publisher is not engaged in rendering accounting,
legal, or other professional advice. If expert assistance is required,
the service of a competent professional person should be sought.

LIBRARY OF CONGRESS CATALOGING IN PUBLICATION DATA
Gill, Michael.
Fired up! : From corporate kiss-off to entrepreneurial kick-off /
Michael Gill & Sheila Paterson.
p.   cm.
ISBN 0-670-86548-6 (alk. paper)
1. Small business—Planning.   2. Entrepreneurship.   3. Self-employed.
I. Paterson, Sheila.   II. Title.
HD62.7.G543   1996
650.1—dc20   95–48990

This book is printed on acid-free paper.
∞

Printed in the United States of America
Set in Melior
Designed by Bonni Leon-Berman
Title page based on jacket design by Jon Valk

For my wife, Elisabeth Childs Gill,
who adds a joyous love to all our lives
—Michael Gill

For my mother, Sarah Agnes (Nessie)
Paterson, who was as "fired up"
as they come—with love,
Sheila Paterson

Contents

Acknowledgments

For Kate Newlin, who introduced us to our agent, Loretta Barrett. For Loretta, who helped make it happen and recommended Mindy Werner as one of the great editors. For Mindy, whose intelligent and graceful editing has consistently improved our manuscript. And for a host of other friends, entrepreneurs, and colleagues too numerous to mention individually, who have supported us with invaluable insights and encouragement. A few who went beyond the call of duty in helping us bring *Fired Up!* to life are: Dianne Marcano, Shannon O'Callaghan, Hillary Hoffenberg, Gary Morris, Tom Keller, Arthur Cohen, Robert E. Jacoby, Don and Erika Robertson, Kim Macalister, Arthur Quinby, Carl Spielvogel, Jim Donohue, Chip and Anne Childs Collins, Elisabeth, Charles, Laura, and Anne Gill, Brendan Larson, Larry Bramble, Florence Peterson, Betsy Lewin, Kevin O'Connor, Louise Schimmel, Louis Salamone, Mike Errecart, Greg Mahnke, Mike Fodor, Marci Miller, Tim Corrigan, Gordon Fenton, Paul Irving, David and Steven Badger, Marilyn Banes, Porter Bibb, Mel Sokotch, John Shaw, Kermit Hummel, Charles Barnard Gill, Rod Perkins, Arlene Curry, Dilys Evans, Peter Becket, Douglas Duchin, and Elke Stone.

You can hardly breathe.

You are sitting in a meeting. Yet another meeting, in a day seemingly filled with them. There are about a dozen people in the room; each, you know with a sinking heart, has something they just have to say. They all are eager, even desperate to speak, encouraged by the dysfunctional form of sibling rivalry indigenous to most companies—they must be heard. And so they talk, and every word they say seems to diminish the supply of fresh air, and fresh ideas.

Your brain begins to go numb, and yet your heart beats faster as you alternate between a kind of frustrated rage—for you would like to be heard and recognized as well—to a kind of fatalistic passivity. In these few meeting-bound minutes you almost grow to hate your fellow workers.

Yet they are not bad people. They are not, by and large, evil people. On the contrary, they are good people, intelligent people, energetic people. Yet the corporate institution encourages this insane situation.

In the busy world of the 1990s, nothing is more precious than time. And here you are—here you *all* are—wasting hours and hours of precious time. You would like to get up and go, yet you know that would be a corporate no-no.

It begins to feel as if someone is literally choking you. Yet you can't move. There doesn't seem to be any alternative. You would like to say something, do something, yet you fear that any impolitic word or act could get you fired. You are trapped. You have never been more frustrated in your life.

The next day, you go to a noted career consultant, a specialist in corporate stress, and he tells you that your choking experience was "quite normal." He says: "Many people in corporations in the nineties experience this choking sensation. It is based on the frustration that many encounter in the corporate world today. They want to get out—yet they don't have the courage to leave. That is their frustration. And it leads to a choking sensation. For they are literally choking off their own best instincts."

On the one hand, you are relieved that you are not alone in having such a frustrating experience. On the other hand, it strikes you with new force that corporate life is not the ideal life for you.

But what to do? You have acquired a serious case of paycheck dependency . . . your whole world is geared to the steady arrival of the biweekly contribution. You have heard that people can be successful on the outside, but you have no idea what it is really like "out there."

You don't really hate your fellow corporate workers, yet it does seem that the whole system is set up to create a zoolike mentality. And you have seen that the more corporations try to reengineer themselves—the more they downsize, rightsize themselves—the more mindless, suffocating meetings seem to result.

And when you add the usual, inevitable amount of corporate politics, the air becomes thin. You feel like you are in an emotional and mental cage. You begin to become claustrophobic, and you yearn to breath free.

You hope to escape from the stifling cage of a corporate employee and experience the joy of taking control of your destiny, deciding where you want to go and what you really want to do. You know others who have escaped and have been rejuvenated by the experience. You wish you knew more about what it was really like outside. . . .

Going from Fear of Being Fired, to Fired Up

We will tell you what it is like to make the move from being fearful of being fired to being *Fired Up!,* working for yourself, with a new freedom enhancing every aspect of your life: to be in charge of your own destiny and empowered with the ability to make your own decisions; to have the potential to have financial rewards without limits.

Once you become an entrepreneur, almost immediately you will lose the old fears and frustrations you had as an employee. But as you let yourself go, you will encounter a whole new roller coaster of powerful emotions. Learning to use this new emotional energy will be a key to your success.

Our book is a guide to what you can actually expect to experience as an entrepreneur. We tell you what it's like to live the life of the entrepreneur and what it will take for you to be successful. In addition to our own experiences, we have talked to over three hundred people who have escaped the corporate zoo and moved from employee to successful entrepreneur. Through their stories we give you real-life experiences from successful entrepreneurs in many different businesses: from the rapidly growing service sector to manufacturing to retail to restaurants to biotech to baking, the full range of extraordinary activities that entrepreneurs are engaged in today.

We will tell you stories of entrepreneurs who are very young and of those who have left after lengthy careers in big corporations, started their own businesses, and become successful beyond their wildest dreams.

We have interviewed entrepreneurs in small towns and big cities in virtually every region of the United States and even in Europe.

In talking with these entrepreneurs and in getting to know them and their stories, we found a clear pattern and common insights about what it's really like to live the entrepreneurial life and what it really takes to succeed.

We have carefully selected the stories throughout our book to dramatize and underscore these key insights and to help you experience the life of the entrepreneur and understand what it takes to succeed.

Joining the Entrepreneurial Revolution

There is an entrepreneurial revolution going on—across America and across the world. More and more, employees everywhere are becoming entrepreneurs at an incredible, historic rate. Many are doing it because of downsizing, restructuring, and ongoing corporate upheavals. Many more are becoming entrepreneurs because of the growing opportunities to chart your own destiny and receive rewards simply impossible under a traditional corporate structure.

An entrepreneur, Kent Black, who has built his own successful business, Kent Black & Associates, advising people on their careers, says: "Ten years ago, people would come in to see me from the big corporations. Their desire then was to find a similar job—at higher pay. Today, it's all so different. There's an entrepreneurial revolution going on. And today people ask me: How can I get a whole new life?"

You may be happy as an employee and yet still dream about a future move . . . you might be fed up and are taking definite steps to leave, or you might have been fired and you're deciding what to do. No matter where you are, you will welcome the truth of what it's really like to be an entrepreneur.

We realize that some people are simply not ready to make a

move. Nevertheless, whether or not you become an entrepreneur, reading our book will make you better prepared and more successful whatever you finally decide to do.

But How to Begin?

We know what you are going through, for we are also escapees from the corporate zoo. We have experienced the feeling of being choked and immobilized—spending too much time fearing what the corporation could do to us—from the fear of being fired (Would we be fired? When would it happen? Could it be avoided? Should we let ourselves be fired and leave gracefully with a generous severance package?) to the fear of going out on our own.

We were two employees who had had successful careers working for billion-dollar international corporations. Each of us really wanted to leave and start our own businesses, but we were afraid. We were trapped between the fear of being fired and the fear of going into our own business. Each of us asked: "Do I have it in me to be an entrepreneur? What is it really like out there? What about the risks involved in starting up? What about those friends of mine who have gone into their own business and are now back looking for corporate jobs? What happened to them? Why weren't they successful? Could I be a success on my own?"

On the other hand, although we were fearful of leaving the corporation, we were dismayed by the utter lack of loyalty to employees shown by today's companies. We knew we had every right to be frightened. Downsizing, relocations, mergers—whatever the reason, it was clear that a corporation offered us no safety and none of the security we had known earlier in our careers.

In an article in *Barron's* magazine, James Challenger sums up what we felt and knew to be true: "Employee allegiance to employers is vanishing as workers understand they're viewed as liabilities rather than assets. . . . The most productive employees . . . jump ship when times are good."

When to Jump . . .

For Sheila, the impetus to become an entrepreneur was the completion of a two-year special assignment working in Asia in which she was virtually running her own business. With the assignment complete, her only alternative was to return to the home office and to the job she had years before. She had no desire to reenter a corporate environment in a job she had already done. Her decision was helped by the fact that her company was still in disarray after a messy merger that threatened to tear the whole organization apart (an event that later occurred after she left). She felt she couldn't go home again. But she was afraid to leave. Then her boss offered her an incredibly generous exit package. Sheila was happy to pick this moment to move on. She knew this opportunity would never happen again.

Mike had planned to be an entrepreneur ever since he began his corporate career. His plan was to work for a major corporation for five years and then go out on his own. But as often happens, he found himself a part of the seductive corporate game of promotions, titles, big offices, and substantial compensation. His impetus to finally jump was the desire to relocate his family from the freeways of LA to the mountain village in New England where he and his wife had grown up. He had come face-to-face with the fact that unless he gave himself a deadline, a specific time to go, he would spend his life talking and dreaming of an entrepreneurial existence without really doing what he wanted to do. When his daughter was due to graduate from sixth grade, he and his wife decided that this was the best time to leave.

In 1990, Mike and Sheila simultaneously left their corporate jobs to found their own, now successful companies. Mike has built his growing company, Michael Gates Gill & Friends, offering creative solutions to challenging marketing problems for such organizations as American Express, Mobil Oil, and the National Football League. Sheila has helped build several international organizations and is now a partner in Macro International, where she offers research and strategic marketing advice to major multinationals such as Mars, Campbell's soup, Pepsi, and Procter and Gamble.

Together, Mike and Sheila are providing entrepreneurial marketing solutions to a select group of clients, ranging from Rembrandt Toothpaste to the Department of Energy.

How Our Book Came About

In 1992, Mike relocated his business to Norfolk, Connecticut, directly across the street from Sheila's home. We began to talk, as entrepreneurs do when they get together to share stories. In talking about our experiences, we quickly realized that we shared many similar lessons on how to be successful. We had discovered that we could tap into emotional and mental capacities that we never thought we had.

Along the way we had made mistakes, and we were frank in discussing them. We realized that many of our mistakes came because we were so surprised by how different life was when you made the move from employee to entrepreneur. There were literally hundreds of surprises. Nobody had told us what it was really like when you leave the corporate zoo for life in the wild.

What Nobody Ever Tells You . . .

None of the books that we had read prepared us for the life of the entrepreneur. Yes, they told us how to write a business plan, how to set up an electronic office, the importance of keeping an eye on our finances—but nobody told us the experience of what it would really be like and what it takes from an emotional standpoint to be successful.

As you make the move from employee to entrepreneur, you will be amazed at how different everything is, and how many surprises you must survive to succeed, of the dramatic transition you must make. Who would have imagined, for example, that one of the biggest challenges facing today's entrepreneur is the ability to handle incredible and early success? This surprising fact almost put Sheila's company out of business. Can you imagine marketing your business like you would a box of Tide—even though you are only a one-person service operation? Do you know that entrepreneurs speak a different language from employees and that this is a language that you had better learn quickly or else?

As an entrepreneur recently told us: "When you leave your corporate job to set up your own business, *everything* is life-threatening. Almost any decision, if it is the wrong one, can sink your new venture." From choosing a partner to an office location, or even a particular accountant, the results can be fatal to your business.

We wondered: *Why hadn't anybody told us what it was really like? And what it really takes to be successful?*

The Big Question: What Is It Really Like "Out There"?

We also shared the fact that many of our friends were always asking what it was really like "out there." A lot of our friends were still employees, yet they were desperately eager to learn what it took to succeed as an entrepreneur. They were surprised by our stories and intrigued. We told them the truth—with a tone of tough love. And they seemed so grateful, and eagerly asked for more information about entrepreneurial life.

We both agreed that we spent a lot of time simply advising our friends—or friends of friends—about what entrepreneurial life is really like. We had even been asked to give speeches to other prospective entrepreneurs to tell them what it was really like.

We decided that there was a need for a book that revealed what it was really like to be a *Fired Up!* successful entrepreneur. More importantly, we wanted other entrepreneurs to avoid the mistakes that we had made.

As we began to develop our book, we decided to interview others and to join our stories with those of many who have moved successfully from employee to entrepreneur.

Stories Never Told

Our heroes all share the common characteristic of being people you can learn from. Our book gives you *practical advice* told in an empathetic, emotional way and *real-life stories* that will help you experience the lessons these entrepreneurs have learned. They are from all ages and backgrounds, but with one similar achievement: These people have turned their entrepreneurial dreams into successful realities.

And you can too.

By the time you have read our book, you will have entered and experienced the secret world of the entrepreneur. Through these shared insights you will learn invaluable lessons about what it takes to be successful.

Our book will transform your life, just as the experience of being an entrepreneur transforms and energizes the lives of more people every day.

But our book is not a textbook. We know you don't have time for that. That's why we purposefully designed our book to be read, for example, on a round-trip airplane ride between New York and Chicago.

Our book can help you make the critical decision to stay or to go.

We also have a quick but brutal test that you should wait until the end of the book to take. This test will help to confirm your decision: Is being an entrepreneur right for you? It isn't right for everybody.

If you pass the test, then we have developed for you a list of eleven steps you can take right now, while you're still an employee, to get you started in the life of the entrepreneur.

We are a man and a woman who are living the entrepreneurial life. We are Fired Up! We are energized entrepreneurs who have achieved our business goals and are living lives that are better than we ever imagined. We are confident that once you read our book, you, too, will have an understanding of the truth of what it really takes to move from a frustrated employee to a successful, Fired Up! entrepreneur. Our battle cry has become "Don't be fed up, get Fired Up!"

The Roller-Coaster Ride of Your Life

"I start the morning feeling that my company is going to crash, and I end the day knowing the company is going to live—it's my biggest emotional high. Day after day is an emotional roller-coaster ride!"

> —*Larry Goodwin, founder and president of Goodwin Manufacturing, a successful entrepreneurial firm in the Midwest*

When you finally leave the familiar routines of the corporate zoo and head out into the wild, dynamic world of the entrepreneur, you will experience an incredible roller-coaster ride of powerful, surging emotions—emotions whose frequency and intensity will take you by surprise.

You will feel a new intensity of anger and frustration, often turning to rage. You will also feel a sense of wild joy in your new freedom, and a kind of ecstasy in your achievements you never thought could ever be such an integral part of your busy business day.

You will feel this range of powerful, primal emotions with dizzying, disorientating frequency. During just one day you will find yourself experiencing the highest highs and the lowest lows—

the cheers and tears that are the moment-by-moment reality of entrepreneurial life.

It is critical for you to be prepared for this emotional roller coaster, and to realize that you are not going crazy when you are taken on this exciting emotional ride—this is the normal experience for *all* entrepreneurs. This holds true no matter what size or kind of business you decide to start. Successful entrepreneurs learn to deal with these emotions and make them work *for* them.

Once you are prepared for the energy of these powerful emotions, you can learn to use it to turn your roller coaster into a fast track that will help you achieve your dreams.

Based on experience and research, we have developed what we call the Rules of the Ride. These will help you to move forward in your entrepreneurial life.

The Rules of the Ride

Expect to Experience a Whole New Feeling of Freedom: The Excitement of an Uncaged Life

You will be astonished when you experience your first morning of freedom and leave your stuffy corporate office—forever—to go out on the street. You will be surprised by how warm the sun feels, how bright the colors look. But even more, you will be surprised by all the *people* out on the street. "What are they doing?" you think to yourself. "Don't they have *jobs?* Shouldn't they be sitting inside, working at their desks, just as I used to do?" Then you will feel a sudden rush of positive adrenaline as you realize now you have the gift of deciding what to *do*—each day. You are free to do as you please—each day. Your sense of freedom will fill you with an overwhelming excitement.

A successful entrepreneur describes her own first morning of freedom this way: "I was driving across the George Washington Bridge—away from Manhattan. I realized—with a kind of awesome, energizing joy—that I could go anywhere and do anything I wanted.

"It was like being let out of school—but to an even greater degree. For I had been planning for years to get out of corporate life—and now I had finally done it. I put the song 'Take This Job and Shove It' on the tape deck and sang it exultantly—along with Willie Nelson.

"I will always recall my sense of liberation. It was confirmation that I was on the right road—at last. I had taken back control of my own life and was free to do what I really wanted with it. You know that famous poem: 'I am the Master of My Fate, the Captain of My Soul'? That's the way I felt my first day of freedom, and every day since."

Everyone who makes a successful move from employee to entrepreneur has those liberating moments they remember as transforming, energizing experiences. Their feeling of freedom strongly validates their decision to move to entrepreneurial life.

Another corporate escapee simply walked out of an important meeting one day and left his overstuffed briefcase on the floor of Grand Central Station. It was as though that one, symbolic act gave him permission to live his life his way. He went back to his hometown in the Midwest and opened up a small manufacturing plant specializing in making luggage designed for business travelers. Today, his plant has grown into a large enterprise.

"I could never have done it," he says, "if I hadn't gotten out of that stifling corporate environment. I'll never forget walking away from my briefcase, just leaving it, and thinking: Now I can live my life the way I always dreamed I could. That sense of freedom is the greatest feeling in the world!"

For those of us who have spent much of our life caged in the corporate zoo, being let out can be exhilarating beyond anything we ever imagined.

"The sky is literally the limit," as one entrepreneur told us.

You will experience a remarkable sense of freedom. And it is important that you value it and remember it, for it is an emotional, elemental confirmation of your decision to go out and become an entrepreneur.

This sense of great freedom and energizing excitement will be the first of many primal emotions that you feel.

Expect to Ride a New Range of Powerful Emotions

One moment you will be yelling, so proud of a great victory. The next moment you might be screaming with rage. Each moment you feel things more strongly than you ever have before. Suddenly your grown-up veneer gives way to a childlike sensitivity that causes you to feel—within minutes—wonderful happiness and acute distress. Your variety of emotions, coming with such rapidity and power, scares you. You wonder if you are going crazy.

The successful entrepreneur Larry Goodwin says that "nobody ever told me that I would have such powerful feelings, and go so quickly from one to another. One moment I will leap for joy, and the next moment I am pounding the desk so hard my arms get black and blue."

What Larry has experienced is true for all entrepreneurs—their emotions are engaged in a way and with an intensity they have never experienced before. As an entrepreneur, you realize with a shock that it is not just your business—it is your *life*. Every new entrepreneur experiences this consuming, emotionally powerful sense of total involvement.

Larry, like many entrepreneurs, has been challenged, and has succeeded. He has increased sales every year since he started his company. But it hasn't been easy—he has had to use every ounce of energy and emotion to make these major changes happen.

You will find yourself riding a wide range of emotion . . .

From Joy . . .

"We literally ran all the way to the bank," an enthusiastic entrepreneur told us. "I was so pleased that someone believed in my business enough to actually give us money—with a check made out to the company name! I couldn't wait to present it to the cashier. I wanted the whole world to know."

To Rage . . .

An entrepreneur in the manufacturing business told us about the first time he got a major order from a key customer. It was an order large enough to transform his business. When he put down the phone, he literally leaped for joy and went running up and down the corridor of his little business giving high fives to his three employees. When he got back to his computer he had trouble processing the order. Then his computer simply quit on him. He went into a towering *rage.* In the old days, in his corporate life, he could complain to someone, but now he realized he had to figure out how to solve this problem *himself.* Which made him even angrier. He got up, looked around, and kicked his wastepaper basket as hard as he could. It felt like he had broken his foot. He let out a *scream.*

To Frustration . . .

A successful entrepreneur says, "Sometimes I get so frustrated I could cry." She told us of a time when "it was minutes before a meeting with a key customer. The office was a mess, and my partner and I still hadn't agreed upon what we were going to offer them. I was so frustrated I started to cry. And crying for me was a big no-no in business life. I had always looked upon crying—especially a woman crying—as a sign of weakness. But now, crying was a necessary relief. And I wasn't embarrassed. It was my business that was in a turmoil, why shouldn't I cry? Who had a better right to cry? So I cried. I cried my heart out. It calmed everyone down. Then I dried my tears, and got to work, and we got the business."

To Terror . . .

There will be those moments of mental and physical exhaustion. An experienced entrepreneur told us: "Sometimes, usually at three o'clock in the morning, you will feel besieged by every possible concern. And you will find yourself swinging between moods of great confidence to bleak despair. Sometimes you have a feeling of pure, undiluted terror. You don't know how your business will ever succeed. You are scared by all the responsibilities you have taken on."

To Exultation

"But the next morning, even as you get out of bed, you are kicked into a confident, positive gear by an irresistible feeling of exultation. You are doing what you wanted, following a life you yourself have designed. You shake your head with wonder at your previous, late-night concerns. In the fresh light of day you are full of confidence and exultation as you prepare to fulfill your dream. You can't believe the swings from joy to despair."

But don't despair. This powerful range of feelings, this emotional roller coaster, is *normal*. This is *healthy*. This is the essential nature of the ride you are on. You are recapturing the spirit and power that is integral to the freedom of the life you have chosen.

You have left the corporate zoo for an entrepreneurial life in the wild. You are discovering the quick and intense reactions that kept our ancestors alive in what was always a challenging environment. And you will feel more *alive* than you ever have before. *The very strength and range of emotions that you feel is an essential attribute and a vital component in the life of any successful entrepreneur.*

So you must learn to appreciate and use your emotions. Which leads to our next rule.

Learn to Trust Your "Intelligent Emotions"

At some time you will probably have an experience that comes down to the fact that you just don't "feel right" about some decision. For example, you might not feel right about going forward with a person who wants to be your business partner. And yet, on paper, he looks irresistible. He has done well before and now wants to invest a large sum of money in your operation. All the rational reasons seem to point to his being an important addition to your business. Yet you feel in your gut that this could be a mistake. Finally, fighting against your emotions, you go forward and take him on as your partner. It is a decision you will regret.

An entrepreneur told us a story of how she lost precious time and valuable forward momentum for her company by fighting against her better instincts. Her first partner seemed to come from central casting. He was handsome, dynamic, with lots of great connections. But on her very first business trip it was clear that he didn't respect her or care to hear her opinions. Instantly she felt that this was a major mistake. Yet she didn't act on her instincts for years. Years that cost her dearly in the growth of her business.

Another entrepreneur made a similar mistake in overriding her emotions. She said that she had been planning for months to leave the large fashion firm where she was working. Her designs were the reason for its success, and she felt that it was time to build a business on her own. But when she told her boss, he convinced her, against her instincts, to stay for "just one more season." Her heart wasn't in it, her designs were not as good as they had been in the past, and that "one more season" was a disaster. So when she did finally go out, after waiting longer than she had felt right about, instead of launching her business from a successful base, she had to go out under a cloud created by a disastrous season.

"It was like a car accident," she now says, "a car accident that didn't have to happen. If I'd just acted on what I felt, I could have had a lot easier time. I should have trusted my instincts."

Peter Salovey, professor of psychology at Yale University, teaches a course on what he calls "intelligent emotions." After many objective and scientific studies he has concluded that emotions are not fuzzy abstractions, but, on the contrary, accurate guides as to what you should really do in your life.

This is especially true when you are on the ride of the entrepreneur. Emotions can help you to hold on to reality, and they can keep you headed in the direction that plays to your greatest strengths.

You have to learn to trust your "intelligent emotions." When you go forward with someone you don't feel good about, or work on a project in which you don't really believe, you could be giving up more than you realize. For time is the most precious resource of any entrepreneur—and time spent on efforts without a strong emotional foundation will not be successful. It is a tragedy to spend time with a person or on an effort you are instinctively not sure of.

When you work with people you don't really trust, on a project you don't really believe in, you are almost bound to fail. When you are working with people you enjoy, doing something that you love, you will find that you can create an incredible forward motion. Remember: The very word *emotion* has motion in it.

A thoughtful entrepreneur says: "The biggest mistakes I make are not following my instincts—particularly when it comes to prospective customers. You do have to like the person you are working with. Without that positive emotion, terrible things can happen."

So we recommend strongly that you use your emotions to help set your compass. They can be an intelligent guide as to which direction you should take.

Learning to check your *internal compass,* rather than external politics, is what distinguishes an entrepreneur from a corporate employee.

Learn to Go from External to Internal Validation

When you do get out and start up your own business, you will undoubtedly have this kind of experience: You are in a meeting with a major customer. He asks you a direct, challenging question. This is a question you would have stumbled over in your previous, corporate life—not sure how your boss or your company would like you to answer. But now, as your *own* boss, you are able to *check your own internal compass,* which points to telling the prospect the truth. So you tell the truth, and you get the sale.

You will experience the speed and ease that comes with saying what you believe and acting on it—rather than being afraid of the opinions of others.

An entrepreneur, who has built a successful international consulting business, tells this story: "As soon as I left the big company I had been working for, I had a chance to make a major presentation to one of their most important customers. Previously, I had always been inhibited when I was involved in such a presentation—for I realized my whole career was riding on how well my boss thought I had done. But when I began to present on my own, I didn't care about my corporate career, I cared about delivering a great idea for a customer. And my new confidence was invaluable in making the sale. My success was a surprise to my corporate colleagues—they were shocked at how effective I could be out on my own—with no support. I felt like the mouse that became a lion."

John Gray, president of Bubbies Pickles of San Francisco, tells a similar story about the difference between listening to your own internal instincts and following the external corporate inhibitions. A banking client of his was representing a failing pickle company. John had been thinking about going into business. The client took him to the store to buy a jar of Bubbies pickles. One taste, and he had a sudden inspiration. He decided he would go into business to sell great pickles. He shared his inspiration with his corporate colleagues.

He told them, "I think I might go into the pickle business." Predictably, his corporate peers burst into laughter. They told him he was crazy.

Their negative reaction was added impetus. He thought to himself: "I will find a way to *do* it!" The "I will find a way to *do* it" attitude has been a positive, emotional catalyst in launching the careers of many successful entrepreneurs.

He left the bank within weeks and today makes the best pickles in America. He is successful beyond his expectations. The reason for his success: "I stopped listening to the corporate types—who didn't really know anything anyway—and started listening to my own emotions. I learned to trust my instincts to help chart my business."

When you become your own boss, it is important, in fact essential, that you look to yourself for *internal validation.* You will have to cure yourself of the dependence on external validation from corporate "heavies" and "higher-ups."

This continuous seeking after a kind of approval, a kind of political popularity, is the single most virulent disease of corporate life. It seems to eat like a cancer at the heart of most large companies. The corporation, perhaps by its size and structure, even by its very *nature,* encourages employees to take a disproportionate interest in the opinions of all other corporate types. This need for endlessly building consensus can blunt bold initiatives and slow actions that should take days into weeks or even months of delay.

The need for validation among corporate colleagues can turn original ideas, with real substance and flair, into the ugly step-children of ideas: concepts that are logical in every detail, that everyone agrees with, but have lost their life, their originality, and even their very reason for being by the very process of gaining acceptance from such a large group.

The sickly, overheated corporate environment also encourages a kind of *meeting mindlessness.* People become more concerned about what their boss will think than about how the market as a whole will react. You often hear the question in corporate corridors: "How did the meeting go?" You seldom hear the question: "What did the meeting accomplish?" Meetings seem to be many companies' most important product.

You will be startled at how quickly you can become unstuck. Simply by getting out of the corporate zoo, your point of view changes. You won't feel the need to socialize every decision until it is worn away to blend in with the bland corporate wallpaper. In fact, your new business will only have a corporate wallpaper that *you* pick out.

You will be surprised at how quickly and effectively you will be able to think, and to act, when you no longer are full of corporate inhibitions.

And you will also be pleased at how fast your confidence in your own judgment increases and how quickly you will be able to react to changing situations. Which is fortunate, for in the life of every successful entrepreneur you have to . . .

Expect the Unexpected

One minute you will be riding along, thinking how well everything is going—and the very next minute you will be plunged into the darkest tunnel. You will never think you can survive, when suddenly you are back out in the bright sunshine, racing forward. The roller-coaster ride of the successful entrepreneur has many such twists and turns.

As a successful entrepreneur, you learn to expect the unexpected, and not to give up when things don't come through as they were promised. For—like the weather—things change quickly for entrepreneurs.

One entrepreneur had been promised—while he was still an employee—that he would be given a lot of business. "This promise was given by someone before I went out," he says. "She had urged me to go out on my own, to start my own company. She said she couldn't wait to support me by giving me some important pieces of business. And then, on that first week when I called, she was busy. When, weeks later, I was finally able to speak with her, she told me blithely that she didn't have anything . . . right now.

" 'Right now!' I said, 'but I need your business right now to survive!'

" 'You promised me,' I told her. She was cool. 'Don't pressure me,' she said, 'I hate to be pushed.'

"I thought, for a few days, that I was done for. I even became so desperate that I thought of returning to corporate life. But then, the unexpected happened . . . on the positive side of the ledger. A big, potential customer called with a major assignment. I didn't know anyone there, but a friend of a friend had said I might be able to help them. Their business turned out to give me that extra lift I needed, and assured me of success."

This entrepreneur's story is not unusual. It is often true in entrepreneurial life that what you expect to have happen, what you have been promised will happen, doesn't; but then, seemingly out of the blue . . . comes even better news. The only way to account for this serendipitous style of life is that there is something in the business cosmos that does, indeed, love an entrepreneur.

Another entrepreneur told us a story of a banking nightmare. He had a manufacturing business to launch—one that required a major capital outlay to get going. The bank had assured him that there would be no problem with the loan. He had based his whole decision on that assurance. But once he had left his secure corporate job and was in the final stages of finalizing the deal, the bank got cold feet. They said that they had not realized how little collateral he really had. They told him they still believed in him, but that the economy had changed, interest rates had gone up, and they would have to restructure the deal. And that restructuring might take months, if it happened at all.

The bottom line was that they could not give him the money he needed when he needed it. (This is not unusual behavior with banks, and we will tell you later on how to take advantage of banks by turning their own practices against them.) He felt like he had just been handed a gun and told to commit business suicide. But he refused the bank's offer of business suicide. Instead, he used their rejection as emotional ammunition and put together an impassioned presentation to a person he expected to be his biggest customer. He told this prospect that he would deliver an unequaled product to him, at a third less than the competition, with one proviso—he needed the money for the order up front. His customer agreed with his proposal and told him that he would be able to give him a contract and also deliver at least six months of potential credit to get him started. The entrepreneur didn't know whether to laugh or cry. He decided to simply smile, express his gratitude, and get to work with new energy.

There is a simple lesson to be learned from such dramatic and continuous changes: Don't overreact.

Learn Not to Panic—at Least Not in Public

You are having lunch with a friend. She congratulates you. She is impressed by how well your business is going. But inside your briefcase you have a letter canceling a major order. You can feel your heart beating. You have to get back to the office. You feel like an impostor, sitting here letting her compliment you on your growing business when you feel, with a kind of terrifying certainty, that it is at this minute crashing to earth. Her compliments seem to make it harder to bear—as though you were a trapeze artist with the crowd applauding as you realized you had made a fatal mistake and were falling to the earth below, without a net. It is hard to believe that you will be able to make something happen to get you out of this terrible mess. You feel like screaming.

Go ahead and scream. It is one of the perks of the entrepreneur. All entrepreneurs do it from time to time, just as you would on a roller coaster. You are moving so fast, both up and down, that if you didn't scream, you wouldn't be normal. So go ahead and scream—but do so when you return to the privacy of your own office. A positive, smiling public face is vital for success as an entrepreneur.

And the smile can be based on a positive belief that will give you energy for forward motion, for you should know that if you keep doing what you feel is right, you will get where you want to go.

A president of a large and successful commercial real estate business tells us that his biggest problem in the beginning was not understanding the way things could change from an enthusiastic "yes!" to a "maybe." He would have a large corporation tell him with enthusiasm that they wanted to close a deal, but months might go by before they even really got down to the details that would make it work. Sometimes it wouldn't happen at all. To him, his life was on the line. To them, it was just another business deal, one of hundreds they were considering.

So you can't count on your potential customers having the same concerns with getting things done. You have to generate the positive energy and just keep going. Your motto should be: "Plan for the worst, expect the best."

We don't know of any successful entrepreneurs who have managed to avoid large disappointments, plans that went awry, people who let them down. But in every case, when they kept going, they were rewarded beyond their greatest dreams.

How do you find the strength to overcome your natural panic and tap into greater, more positive emotional resources? Read on.

Learn to Value and Tap into the Three Key Emotions of Entrepreneurial Life, and Your Success Is Assured

These three are determination, passion, and the desire to create something new.

First we will deal with the absolute importance of unyielding determination—for without determination your dreams cannot come true.

As an entrepreneur, it is inevitable that you will be buffeted from side to side as you experience the roller coaster. Sometimes you will think that the easiest thing is just to let go—and let yourself be thrown off. But you must hang on. You have to focus with a kind of relentless determination on keeping your grip. And your determination to hang on will help you get where you want to go.

In our experience, and in the experience of all entrepreneurs we've talked to, the single most important quality in their success is: *determination*. Most new business failures occur within the first year, so if you can stay on the ride, your odds dramatically increase that you will be successful.

"I am the quintessential determined person," Judith Ets-Hokin says. "After my divorce, as a single mother with three kids and bill servers at the door, I had to be determined to build my business. And I was. And I *am*."

Judith is founder of HOMECHEF, the unique cooking school and cookware store dedicated to the home chef that is now expanding nationally and internationally. Judith has become known for demystifying and sharing the secrets of the world's great chefs and making them understandable, easily available, and usable in the home. "Anyone can cook a great meal—in minutes," Judith says. "It is a question of the right techniques and the right equipment. In my schools I give people the knowledge and the confidence so that they can add a degree of excellence to the most natural and enjoyable occasions in their lives.

"HOMECHEF seems like such an obvious idea for a successful business now," Judith says, "but there were many times during the early days that I could have given up. My very first location for my school was a terrible one. I was naive. I didn't even have room for parking. I had to rent a driveway across the street. I had to park the cars of the people who came to the class myself.

"But I never thought of giving up. And I didn't sell out when I became more and more successful. Once, Macy's called because they had heard of me. They offered me a job conducting classes in thirteen of their stores. It could have been quite remunerative. But when I went to the meeting at Macy's, it was full of very serious and aggressive people, and they all spent a lot of time referring to Macy's as though Macy's itself were some kind of deity. I still remember leaving the meeting. There was a labyrinthine corridor. I almost panicked. For a moment, I didn't think I'd be able to find my way out. I still remember the freedom I felt when I reached the street."

Judith has published several books, appeared on TV shows, and has been the subject of many magazine and newspaper articles.

"As I have become more well known and successful, people often come up to me and tell me that they want to go out and build a business of their own. And I tell them they have to have *determination.* Then many say: 'I will give it a year or two.'

"My heart just sinks when I hear that. You can't approach creating anything with that kind of limited attitude. You have to be determined to do whatever it takes—for however *long* it takes—to be successful. You have to have staying power."

Judith has built HOMECHEF into a successful business, but it has not been an overnight success. Judith has spent over two decades building her business. She has graduated over twenty thousand students from her schools. "You can prepare a meal in your own kitchen—simply and quickly—that is the equal in excellence to the greatest restaurant in the world. That is an idea and an experience that I am *determined* to share with people," Judith says.

When You Add Passion and Creativity to Determination—You Cannot Fail

You will discover that when your back is to the wall, you can sometimes be at your bravest and most creative. When it is *your* business on the line, you will call upon resources not only of *determination,* but also of *passion* and *creativity,* you never knew you had. There is something about battling for your own business life that will, indeed, bring out the best in you.

Talent alone won't do it. Brains are important—but there are a lot of brainy people sitting on park benches trying to solve the problems of the universe while life just passes them by.

Popularity is nice, but this is no popularity contest.

Almost all successful entrepreneurs were advised by friends and business associates to let go at some point—usually at the very turning point, when things looked their worst, but were just going to get better.

So determination is vital. But what does determination grow out of? It grows out of doing something that you genuinely *love.* Doing something you feel passionate about. You cannot fake the kind of determination we have talked about . . . the will to continue against all odds.

An entrepreneur we talked to illustrates the crucial importance of doing something you really love. He carefully planned his exit from corporate life. He saved enough to invest in an already up-and-coming business. He thoroughly researched many business opportunities. Finally, he picked a field that he thought would continue to grow in the future: the office market for temporaries.

And he was right. The office market for temporaries has continued to grow.

But he did not grow with it. He discovered—after only six months of doing it—*that he didn't like anything about the actual business he was in.* He had loved the process of *planning* to set up the business—but he didn't love doing the actual work of the business. The very act of supplying temporaries to companies bored him. He didn't like the things he had to do each day, such as interviewing possible temporaries and talking to companies about them.

"I made the mistake of planning to do a job I couldn't enjoy," he now says. "It was like someone planning to play a lot of golf who had never played golf before.

"I discovered I really hated the kind of business I was in. So I got out. Quickly. I felt it was such a mismatch that it was better to get out sooner rather than later.

"It cost me fifty thousand dollars. But it was a lesson worth learning. I went back to working in a business I knew I already really liked. A business I already knew I was good at. And since I've gone back to doing something I love, I've done extremely well. So my advise is: Choose a business that is based on something you love to do. You've got to have a *passion* for your profession."

Love—passion—is an emotion that keeps all entrepreneurs going.

Great determination only occurs when there is great passion. Passion and determination are both keys to having a successful entrepreneurial ride. So you'd better be sure—before you risk your life in a particular business—that you really enjoy being in it, every day.

But there is one more quality, a third key, that is equally important. And that is to be *creative* about handling the challenges life will give you. Strong determination to break through a wall is greatly aided by the imagination to see that you might be able to go around the wall, or leap over the wall entirely.

That kind of creativity is needed to keep you going, to get past the first, inevitable roadblocks you will encounter. (We will be sharing some stories about successful creativity under stress throughout this book—especially in our chapter entitled "The Courage to Make Big Promises—and the Will to Deliver on Them.")

Determination is the result of *passion,* and is made most effective when linked to a talent for being *creative* in a crisis.

With these three keys, you cannot fail. It is just a question of how high you will go.

Of course, that doesn't mean that the ride will easy or ever be dull. In fact, we can promise: You will never be bored again.

The Corporate Zoo Doesn't Prepare You

After the first few years as an entrepreneur, you will get more used to the ride. But, despite all your precautions and growing experience, you will still be surprised by the bumps and turns of the roller coaster of the entrepreneur. It is the nature of entrepreneurial life itself. It is the difference between the corporate zoo and life in the wild. But when you go out, you will be better able to survive the highs and the lows because you are prepared to encounter them and realize what it's really like and what it really takes to succeed on the exciting business ride you have chosen. And you will discover a wonderful fact: *The longer you are on the ride, and the more you learn to use your emotions, the more you can use the roller coaster to move your business forward.*

There will always be twists and turns in having your own business. But as you grow in confidence, and experience, you will be able to realize your full potential. You will discover that you can survive in the wild, despite the lack of preparation that your corporation gave you.

In the corporate zoo you are rewarded for suppressing your feelings. You receive three steady meals a day if you don't growl or leap about or show your emotions—and yet these very emotions are the ones that will help you to be successful in the real world.

In the corporate world you learn to censor your strongest feelings; as an entrepreneur, your powerful emotions will not only be helpful—but invaluable. The better you know them, the more you can use them, the more successful you will be. You will have a whole range of powerful emotions to call on: a feeling of freedom, exultation, determination, creativity, passionate love—even fear. Fear is the emotion we all most fear. Yet we will show you in our next chapter how you can turn the powerful emotion of fear to your advantage. We will show you how worriers make winners.

Worriers Make Winners

Fear Is the Fuel That Can Help Make an Entrepreneur a Success

"I worry when I'm not worried."

—*Martin Braid, successful software entrepreneur of SQL Works, Inc.*

You are sitting in your office, and your hand is shaking as you read the memo announcing a new corporate restructuring. There have been rumors for months, but now it is official. And your life is about to be turned upside down. Once again.

It is like a grown-up game of musical chairs. The music of reorganization or restructuring starts, you and your peers scramble for the chairs, and there are always one or two who don't get to sit down in an office again and are escorted from the party.

And you don't like feeling that your life has become one childish corporate game after another.

You take the memo and squeeze it into a tiny ball that you attempt to throw into your wastepaper basket in the corner of your little office. You miss. To you, this is a bad omen.

You want to shout out the lines from the movie *Network*: "I am mad as hell, and I'm not going to take it anymore!"

Then you shake your head as you realize, with a sense of

pained wonder, that you have become more worried about internal politics, and all the silly moves it implies, than you have about doing a great job.

Worry About Becoming Institutionalized

You realize with a new sense of urgency that it is time to get out before you become *institutionalized.*

Institutionalized is when you worry more about the *internal process* of the corporate zoo than you do about producing any particular product or service for the real world outside.

Institutionalized means that you have passed the point of balance—that you have become unbalanced by the corporate process.

How can you tell if you are institutionalized? Ask yourself if you worry more about the *process* than the product or service you are producing.

The process includes such things as promotions and titles and size of offices and, yes, new bosses or personnel moves that seem to affect your internal destiny.

Most of us have a kind of *secret scale* in our corporate careers, a balance between pain and gain. It is important as you read this book to weigh your anxieties to see where you are in the "should I stay or should I go?" continuum.

Meanwhile, here is one vital sign to look for:

The most important sign that you are ready to leave the confines of the corporate zoo is your realization that you are worrying about the wrong things. If you worry about becoming institutionalized, you are on the way to becoming a winner.

A tiger in a zoo paces up and down the cage and can worry like crazy about a ball of string. So can a person caged in corporate life begin to assume huge anxieties about petty annoyances.

Worrying about the wrong things can not only tie your stomach up in knots, it can tie your life in a tangle. You can become a passive victim of situations that are far beyond your control. Worrying about the wrong things is worrying about things that don't matter, or things that you can't change.

Worrying about the right things is what makes a successful entrepreneur.

The Difference Between Being a Worrywart and a Worry Winner

A corporate worrywart is someone who wastes worries and builds up a fever for no good reason.

An entrepreneurial worry winner focuses on issues that can really make a difference in his or her business life.

And worry can work wonders in helping you find solutions to entrepreneurial challenges. Worry can be the fuel that can power entrepreneurial success.

We have a confession to make: We were both once worrywarts. We worried about all sorts of internal corporate nonsense—before we left. We worried about titles and offices and whether or not our bosses really liked us. Or whether or not *their* bosses didn't say hello to us because they were angry with us, or because they simply didn't notice us (both bad reactions to our eager, smiling presence).

We even spent anxious months worrying about whether we should leave or not. It was a worry that became our major worry. We didn't know then that worrying about whether or not to leave was a *good* sign, that worrying about becoming terminally institutionalized was a sign we were on the road to becoming a worry winner.

But that did not mean that we stopped worrying. Far from it.

When we went out and started our own business, we worried with a *passion* and *intensity* that eclipsed any of our worries before. But now, as liberated entrepreneurs, we were worrying in a way leading to a positive *release,* for we could act in a constructive way about our worry. We came to rely on our worry as you would an invaluable, "tough love" friend.

For worry is a natural and an invaluable emotion. A helpful asset. They always tell you in corporate life: "Don't worry about it." And that is good advice *when you are still inside the corporate zoo.*

For there is no point in worrying about things that are outside your control. And when you are working for a large corporation, most major decisions are often outside your control. Mergers and acquisitions are often decided by two or three people behind closed doors. And so are most major decisions.

But there really is nothing to be gained by worrying while working for a major corporation because *someone else is doing the flying.* Many people in corporate life adopt a defensive style—and simply see themselves as passive passengers on a long, corporate journey.

But when you become an entrepreneur, you are flying your own plane, and worry becomes one of your most important ways to succeed.

As soon as you leave the stultifying corporate environment and take the controls into your own hands, you will find that you are worrying about the right things—things that can dramatically affect your survival and your success.

What are the *right* things to worry about? How can you tell if you are a corporate worrywart, having caught the infectious institutional disease of worrying about internal nonsense, or a worry winner on the path to entrepreneurial success?

In researching this emotion with successful entrepreneurs, we discovered that there are worries that make winners, worries that are signs of entrepreneurial health. These are worries that should be ticking over more or less constantly. Entrepreneurs run at a high worry temperature. But their worry is focused like a hot, illuminating light in the right ways.

Here are the kind of worries that work to make entrepreneurial winners:

What Winners Worry About

"I worry that I might not accomplish anything today. That is my biggest nightmare."

Worrying about *achieving,* rather than simply getting along in a corporate world, is the single most important characteristic of all successful entrepreneurs.

The Young Presidents Club, a group of people that must succeed in becoming president of a major company by the time they are forty to obtain membership, did a study. It was to determine the most important characteristic that accounted for their early success.

They found that the Young Presidents had an extraordinarily high concern with future achievement—versus relaxing in comfort with what they had at present. They were always worrying about achieving more, and willing to postpone pleasure, an easy life, being with family and friends, even popularity, to achieve their long-term goals. In sum: The Young Presidents' strongest characteristic was a willingness to sacrifice present pleasure for the gain of a future goal. They were masters at delayed gratification. *They were always worrying about achieving some ambitious goal in the future, rather than simply sitting back and enjoying the moment.*

While this quality could drive some of their friends and spouses crazy, this constant worry about achieving was also the secret to their success.

Martin Braid, a successful entrepreneur we talked to, is a software consultant much in demand. He lives in one of the most beautiful parts of the country. He has already achieved a high measure of financial success. *If he were not a winner, he might now relax.* He must generate all his own internal discipline against the possible inclination to lie back and enjoy his good fortune. Fortunately, he has a high worry temperature, focused on the right area: reaching a goal he has set.

No matter how late he gets up or how many interruptions in his day, he *makes sure he accomplishes at least one specific objective each day.*

And he employs an excellent technique: He sets his objective the night before so as not to let any external forces disrupt his plans.

The major difference between an employee and an entrepreneur is this ability to set your own goals and achieve them.

An employee must, by the very nature of the situation, respond to the agenda of the company. *Setting your own agenda can move you from the status of a frustrated victim into a satisfied victor.*

Becoming an achiever, rather than simply a part of a process, is the key to success as an entrepreneur. And that means that your worry, your concern, should be focused on achieving *your* goals, rather than pleasing a process set in motion by some other institution.

Worriers who worry about achieving their goals are sure to be winners.

"When I go into a tricky corner, I don't step on the brakes—I step on the gas."

Race car drivers are, by their very nature, entrepreneurs. They have their very survival, as well as their business, riding on four wheels.

Tim Moser, a young entrepreneur, has chosen this demanding field to succeed in. "Obviously, it takes a special kind of worry for such an entrepreneur to survive, and to succeed," Tim says. "Most racetrack entrepreneurs I know nurture a special sort of fear: one that inspires action. The ideal fear is one that leads to a positive response. *Fear that leads to forward motion.*"

He says that "everyone is afraid. It is how you use that powerful emotion that distinguishes the winners from the losers."

A comprehensive study done a few years ago focused on what particular quality was shared by winning race car drivers. This study was commissioned by a major corporation that wanted to invest in people who had the propensity to cross the finish line first.

Researchers discovered that successful drivers came from every socioeconomic background. Some had been born rich, some had struggled up from the bleakest form of poverty. Some were loud and gregarious extroverts. Others were quite shy. And, yes, they were all fearful: They were constant, natural worriers—or they wouldn't have made it to the major race car circuit in the first place. But there was one quality that the winners all shared. It was an innate character trait. They all reacted to their fear in a similar way.

Though all drivers were worried about going into a particularly tricky corner, the losers downshifted to cut their speed and ease their fears, while, on the contrary, the successful drivers *stepped on the gas.* The winners were just as concerned as the losers, but it was their reaction to their worry that was different. For winners, worry is reason to take some *positive action.*

For losers, worry is a signal to step back. Winners move forward—aggressively.

To be successful on the racetrack of the entrepreneur, you must use your fearful conjectures as positive motivators to help you focus on future solutions, and encourage you to *act.*

When you start to worry, remember this fact: Fear is the fuel that makes the entrepreneurial person a success.

You must use that fear, as you would a high-octane fuel, for fast forward motion.

We stress the importance of forward motion because the lesson learned in some corporations is just the reverse: Few are fired for doing nothing, while those that move forward are often criticized. Once outside, on the other hand, you are rewarded for worrying in a creative, action-oriented way.

"I hate to worry about the past. Because there is nothing I can do about it. I worry about the future. Because that worry helps me to survive—when a lot of other people in my profession won't."

Jerry Mink, M.D., is chairman of Tower Imaging, one of the most highly respected and successful radiology operations in the world. "I grew up in a blue-collar neighborhood in Chicago," he says. "I worked hard to become a good doctor and make contributions to my profession." Jerry is the author of several books on radiology and delivers lectures nationally and internationally. "But I realized several years ago—even though I had become very successful by almost every measurement—that if I didn't keep worrying and planning for the future, I wouldn't be able to succeed in the future.

"Today, I spend a lot of time on making sure that our organization is managed as productively as possible: for our hospitals, and the patients they serve.

"I worry constantly that we are doing things that will mean we will be able to offer the highest quality medical advice, in the most effective way for the people that need our support.

"My wife, Barbara, will tell you that I worry *constantly.* I worry about the future. No matter how well we are doing—and we are doing very well—or how much recognition I personally receive, my wife will tell you that I am never at ease.

"I come home at night and spend time worrying about what might happen *next,* and how I, and my colleagues, can do a better job *tomorrow.*

"Medicine is *changing.* The whole world is changing. And if you don't worry about those changes, anticipate those changes, and figure out how you can still provide great quality medicine, then I believe you will be left behind. Doctors who don't worry about the future, won't have a future."

Future worry is a good concept for you to hold on to as an entrepreneur. For we all have a certain amount of anxiety—no matter what kind of life we choose. Doctors or educators, manufacturers or communicators—every field is changing rapidly. It is good to take this free-floating anxiety and anchor it by planning positive moves for the future.

And it is also good to think in terms of what bad things could happen. Think and plan for worse-case scenarios, the toughest possible challenges.

In corporate life, you are primarily surrounded by critics— people eager to point out the error of your ways and the inaccuracies of your ideas. While these corporate critics can drive you crazy, like a swarm of gnats, they do fulfill at least the negative role of making you think through your ideas. Unfortunately, like bugs, they often force you to take your ideas back inside and not let them live outside in the marketplace at all.

But when *you* go outside, you will be freed from these corporate critics. Which is good. As long as you treasure your ability to worry through every idea. Not in a negative way, the way many corporate critics do, trying to defend their territory or their perceived agendas. But worry in a positive way to make sure that you have considered every possible problem that could occur. *That does not mean you worry about the validity of your idea, but rather about how to accomplish it.*

And that is the key distinction. In corporate life, you spend a lot of time defending your ideas, often until they simply disappear. Once outside, you should believe in your ideas, and focus your worry on *how to achieve them.*

Just as a pilot checks the weather before she takes off, or a good surgeon anticipates every possible reaction to any operation, so you must be an excellent worrier in favor of saving and succeeding with your idea. When you worry about everything that can possibly go wrong—well in advance, you can prepare the way for your success.

Then all your surprises can be happy ones.

"I worry until I get it right."

Christopher Little is one of the world's great photographers and has been a successful entrepreneur for many years. One of his greatest strengths is that "I never stop worrying."

Christopher worries about his work. He wants to make sure that each photograph has the originality, the style, and the power to arrest attention that he is expected to deliver. That is not an easy achievement in the creative world of photography. Coming up with that original touch is very rare.

Yet Christopher has used his creative worry to stay at the top of the photographic world. Being that successful takes a lot of hard work.

And takes a lot of worry.

Most successful entrepreneurs are hard on themselves, in the sense that they are never easily satisfied. They have, almost as a birthright, a *restless dissatisfaction with the status quo*. And this dissatisfaction is applied with relentless vigor to their own efforts. They are, like Christopher Little, never content to rest on the success they have built yesterday. They are always focused on what they can do tomorrow.

It is this worry to get it right, and to exceed their own personal expectations that lies at the heart of many entrepreneur's success.

Once again, this is very different from the corporate employee, who often must be more focused on pleasing a boss than getting it right. Being a champion for getting it right, when your boss is telling you to slow down, can get you in serious trouble, even endanger your corporate career. People who fight to get it right can, in a please-the-boss-at-any-cost corporate environment, acquire the reputation as troublemakers. Being a "troublemaker" is not the way to advance quickly up the corporate ladder, where each rung is dependent on the support of others—especially those above you.

Many corporations settle for second-best ideas and advance second-best people in the cause of corporate harmony. The urge to get it right can get you fired.

But as an entrepreneur, you must worry—constantly—that you are living up to *your* expectations. That worry will make you a winner in the marketplace. You must worry about getting it right, for yourself.

And for your customers.

"I worry so my customers don't have to."

Jim Brewster, an entrepreneur who has built a successful printing business called The Formsman, Inc., says: "At three o'clock in the morning I'm often worrying about some customer's job. And my customers know it. Which means that they can get a good night's sleep when they give me a job."

If you worry about your customers—make sure they know it. There is nothing customers love more than hearing that you are worrying about them.

A lot of corporate time is devoted to impressing an internal audience. Successful entrepreneurs focus on pleasing the external market—the customers of the product or service they are offering.

If you are worrying about your customers, you have the right focus for success. No customers ever complained that you worried about them *too much.*

"I like to work with worriers—people who have the strength of character never to be content with the cheap laugh or the easy thrill."

We asked Caryn Mandabach how she has helped build an extremely successful production company in Hollywood. She says that she only hires people who "know how to worry."

"I don't mean worry in the sense of fretfulness," Caryn says, "but rather in the Old English meaning of the word: 'diligence of effort' in the sense of a group of people crafting a beautiful tapestry. To achieve that kind of art, you have to pay attention with a kind of focused, creative energy that adds a whole new dimension to any experience.

"To become a successful entrepreneur it is not a question of personality. It is a question of *character.* You have to have a character that is confident enough to work hard enough over a long enough period to really achieve something original.

"I like to work with people who are always trying to come up with new ideas, new twists. People who can take a good idea and worry until it's even better.

"I'm not looking for a relaxed group, but I expect a positive combustion from all this effort. Our shows are supposed to make people laugh and even cry. To do this, we have to be sensitive and aware of the reality of the world, and yet add a surprising new way of seeing things. That takes a lot of concentrated effort. A lot of strong characters."

Our research and our own experience have shown that the intense activity, concern, and commitment that Caryn Mandabach has described provide the necessary environment for all new ideas.

The history of great ideas is that they usually occur in an incredibly stimulating environment in which every idea is up for challenge. The history of "breakthroughs" in almost every field is a history of lucky accidents that lead to unexpected results. These "accidents" happen most frequently when people are working with other worriers.

Working with worriers is a winning formula. (Just think for a moment of the reverse: Imagine a group of self-satisfied, complacent types. Now how many breakthrough ideas do you think they'd come up with?)

Once again, the key distinction here is that these are not the professional terminators of ideas that many corporations have prowling the halls. For an idea can turn to dust or magic, depending on the talent that rubs against it.

But worriers are people eager for the idea to grow and succeed, and their worry is focused on how to make an idea better, rather than how to bury it. Work with worriers who are focused on *how to make ideas grow,* and you are working with winners who can help make you a winner.

"The biggest mistake I ever made was when I didn't worry enough."

One entrepreneur told us that "winging it is the worst waste of time. When you go in trying to wing it, you can be shot down like a duck."

He tells the story of working for months to set up a meeting with a friend who had a potential to become a major customer. He was so sure that he had a great idea for his friend he didn't even bother to rehearse. He had told his prospective customer that they would have a "relaxed meeting." More of a conversation than a presentation.

Unfortunately, the customer had invited a half dozen other people into the meeting, and they were underwhelmed by the "relaxed" style of the presentation. Their response: He was a sloppy businessman who didn't care enough to present professionally. Result: No order.

The lesson here is that, in entrepreneurial life, nothing is casual and every potential customer should be taken seriously. In fact, most successful entrepreneurs get used to treating virtually everyone they meet as a possible piece of business. And they take every second of opportunity seriously. They worry enough to make every encounter—chance or not—count.

Many talented, articulate, energetic people become entrepreneurs. But only those who worry—and never wing it—really succeed.

"Success is nine-tenths failure."

"What I worry about," says a successful fashion designer, "is *not* failing. Each season I hope to have a couple of items that are total failures. If I don't, I know I haven't pushed it far enough."

Worry about *not* failing. Not failing means that you might have fallen into a comfortable pattern. And a comfortable pattern quickly becomes an uncomfortable rut.

There is something about human nature that makes us better learners when we fail. And being a successful entrepreneur is all about learning—constant learning.

So look upon your failures as the price you pay to continue your education, and assure your success.

"I worry about business timing—all the time."

Lambros J. Lambros, who created Norfolk Holdings, Inc., one of the most successful oil companies of its kind, was frustrated when he was an employee working for a big corporation.

"We often got into something too late," he says, "by the time we had identified a good and profitable category—all the world had piled into the pool.

"When I went out on my own, I was able to move much more quickly and effectively. I created my own oil business, built it, and sold it—all within a matter of a few years. Flexibility, speed, and the ability to act on your idea, *to worry enough to act quickly enough to make it a success,* are what helps to make the successful entrepreneur."

Another entrepreneur, John Childs, has built a successful investment business by knowing when to invest and when to sell out of entrepreneurial ventures.

John helped put together a group of investors to buy Snapple— before it was distributed nationally. John saw high potential in the company. Snapple's unique idea—at the time—was to offer freshly made iced tea with the best ingredients. Snapple was advertised as made from "the best stuff on earth."

Shortly after John and his colleagues purchased the company,

Snapple was able to gain national distribution. The more people tried it, the more they liked it. Suddenly, before the competition could react, Snapple was in stores all across the country. It became a phenomenon, especially with the younger consumers.

Snapple was such a huge hit, it attracted the attention of the "big boys." Nestlé and Pepsi and others piled into the freshly made iced tea area.

John realized that his early investment was now being dramatically challenged by increased competition from copycats— but copycats with deep pockets. Big corporations have a habit of getting into a trend late and then trying to make up for their slowness by spending incredible sums of money.

John and his investors and the original entrepreneurs who built up the Snapple business decided that it was time to sell out to a larger company with more resources and experience in competing with such megasized organizations.

They realized that for Snapple to continue to succeed, it would need an even larger company behind it. John helped orchestrate a sale to Quaker, a company that had the resources and experience needed to help Snapple compete at such a time.

"It was time," John says, "to move on." As an entrepreneur, timing could be on his side. He could make *timely* decisions.

He had no corporate structure to sustain, no major office buildings or sales force to keep going. Above all, he didn't have to take on the incredibly time-consuming task of building a corporate consensus.

He was able to move rapidly on to his next, successful idea.

Today, John is regarded as one of the most astute investors in the world and is busy investing in other companies to give them a chance to grow and reach their full potential, and giving other investors the chance to profit from that growth.

"As an entrepreneur, I worry about spending any money that won't pay off for my business."

When living high on the corporate hog, you learn to spend as much as possible. It becomes one of the corporate perks.

First-class travel, fancy resorts, long meals in luxurious restaurants become a way for you to "get back" some of the often unrecognized effort you put in to the corporation you give so much of your life to.

Consciously or unconsciously, you begin to look forward to opportunities to spend thousands of corporate dollars. It almost becomes a badge of rank, a kind of corporate status. The bigger the expense account, the more you are valued. Or at least that becomes part of your behavior.

You are giving this unfeeling corporation so much, why not grab what you can in expense-account-paid perks?

Why not? Life in the corporation can be bad enough to justify any indulgence you can gain. Any revenge you can take against the corporate "penny-pinchers."

But once outside, when you are spending your *own money,* you will quickly realize that the emotional pleasure, whatever it was, of flying first class and enjoying such expensive perks no longer applies.

You would rather spend that money to advance your ideas and make sure your business is a success.

You find yourself flying coach, and staying at the most reasonable hotel in town. You gain a whole new sense of financial responsibility the moment you leave the corporate expense account behind.

Recently, a successful entrepreneur took a plane to London to set up one of the international seminars that was a specialty of his company. In the departure lounge, he had run into several colleagues whom our friend had known from the days when he worked at the top of a major international corporation. They were still working for the corporation. He agreed to get together on the flight.

He took his seat in coach, and after an hour or so began to look for them. They were clearly not in coach. He smiled to himself. He had even felt guilty about buying his coach fare because it was $740, a couple of hundred dollars more than if he had planned far in advance and accepted some rigid restrictions.

Where could they be? he wondered to himself. He knew from his own experience that the large corporation he had worked for had cut out all first-class fares—for everyone. Yet he couldn't believe they had bought a business-class ticket. He had considered business class himself, until he heard the price: $3,950. More than five times the price of coach. Over three thousand dollars more to spend a few hours on slightly wider seats, sipping some "free" champagne.

When he got off the plane, he caught sight of his friends again. He couldn't resist asking them: "Did you really fly business class?"

"Sure," they said. "Why not? The company policy says we can't fly first class, but we can fly business class on any trip over a thousand miles, even if it doesn't make any business sense!" They all burst into laughter, elated by having a chance to take advantage of the company accountants, and what they regarded as their attempts to rein in their freedom.

He walked away, smiling. But he was smiling for a different reason. He realized that he had been freed forever from any attempts at such childish greed—a greed born of a need for revenge against a company you didn't really enjoy working for. "The company's policy!" What a battle cry of revenge by those who felt ill-used by the corporate system.

He realized with a glow of pride that he now had his *own*

company, he was in charge of his own destiny, and that all the money he spent was a form of investment in himself and his company—such as a trip to London to put on a seminar. He had no need to take revenge against the "powers that be." He had empowered himself!

And along with this new sense of self-empowerment came a real understanding of financial responsibility, and even a feeling of pride in dealing with money in a way that made sense and helped achieve his goals.

For, once you run your own business, you not only gain a new awareness of financial issues, you also gain a whole new sense of financial pride. As an entrepreneur, you see yourself no longer as an embattled corporate victim, but rather as a productive, proactive person, and you take great satisfaction from every dollar you earn.

Mike well remembers the first check he received made out to Michael Gates Gill & Friends, his marketing consultancy. He didn't frame it and hang it on the wall (it was too large not to cash), but he did have a little ceremony, calling in the staff to see his first results. And he did keep the check stub in his wallet like a picture of his kids.

Money becomes something you can be proud to earn—the old-fashioned way, by your talents applied in the manner you have discovered is the most profitable for yourself and your clients.

Money becomes personal. Each check, each dime, has a certain weight.

You worry about money in the positive sense that you are always planning and thinking of ways to make it a more productive and helpful element in your life. You gain in self-respect as you stop *spending* other peoples' money, and begin *investing* your own. Your worry about money takes on a whole new, positive dimension once you see, as you do as soon as you start your business, what an important element in your success it will be.

Above all, money becomes something you don't treat as currency you are *given* in a paycheck, but rather as something you worry about to make sure you *earn.* There is also the joy of *investing money in yourself.* There is no greater reward. When all your worry, and your investment, pays off. It is certainly better than any horse race, or any other gambling, when the odds are never in your favor.

Someone once told us that they asked Ted Turner if he weren't worried about investing all his money in his own business: "I don't worry about that," he said, "I'm betting on myself."

Which leads to our next point . . .

"I worry about keeping fit. The life of the entrepreneur is not a hundred-yard dash—it's a marathon in which proper pacing really pays off."

"When I first got out of corporate life," Sheila says, "and opened my own business I completely ignored my own health. I was so focused on setting the business up, I forgot I was a key to the whole business. I gave up going to the gym, or really getting any exercise—except running for a plane. Then, after too many late nights and late flights brought on by a crazy schedule that allowed me no time to do anything but work, work, work—I got sick with a serious virus. It was difficult for me even to continue to do any work. And I discovered one irrefutable fact: As an entrepreneur *I couldn't afford to get sick.* It's not like a staff corporate job, when you can miss a week or two without worry. My business almost went under.

"I realized then that by not worrying about myself and my

health, I had endangered my business. So from that moment, I've made sure I take good care of myself."

Successful entrepreneurs worry about themselves. They realize that they are important, *the most important element in the success of their business,* and they make sure that they give themselves every chance to succeed.

It all starts with their health.

Most successful entrepreneurs these days make a habit of exercise and eating well. And scheduling meetings in ways that can help them pace themselves.

As a hardworking, successful entrepreneur told us, "It's hard to think well if you've just gotten back from Japan with a terrible cold. I've got to make key decisions every day. I treat myself as you would a beautiful new car. I take care of myself."

Any successful entrepreneurial venture starts with making sure that the entrepreneur is in the best possible mental and physical health. To win or even finish any marathon, you have to train, adopt smart, healthy habits, and generally stay in excellent shape.

Your health is worth worrying about, and doing something about, every day.

"I worry that I will be lost in the crowd."

One of the most important worries for any new entrepreneur is to make sure that you are offering a *unique* product or service, something that answers a genuine need in the marketplace, something that will stand out in the crowd.

Everything from the name you give your business to the look of your business card can affect your success. Which is what our Chapter 8, entitled "You've Got to Be a Brand," is about. But there are some worries even closer to home.

"I worry about having my office in my home."

Many entrepreneurs start with a dream of having a home office. Yet it is *wise* to worry about the idea of having your office in your home. A home office could be a handicap or a help—depending on how you handle it. Which is what our next chapter is all about.

How to Make Your Home a Hell

A Home Office Is an Oxymoron—Unless You Learn How to Separate Your Work Life from Your Home Life

It seems like such a good idea—a home office. This fantasy takes on extra power as you struggle through another long commute to your office. Wouldn't it be wonderful, you think to yourself as you are stuck in traffic or your train is late again, to fall out of bed in the morning, grab a quick cup of coffee, and head to your office . . . in your own home?

Wouldn't it be great, you add, your confidence building, to be able to spend all that time you waste in nonsense meetings in hermetically sealed offices to be at home instead—far from the counterproductive office politics—actually doing the work you love to do?

And isn't the idea of working at home a perfect match for to-day's technology? Can't you simply set up your computer, your printer, your phone, and your fax and be in business? In fact, you have probably read about some of the new technology that has been designed just for this new SOHO—small office, home office—market.

Haven't you seen magazine articles that profile successful entrepreneurs who have done it just that way?

You think of the fact that you have an extra bedroom—couldn't you convert that to a home office and save on the rent?

Yet—despite the ease with which you think you can create a home office—it is important to pause a moment. For this is a fateful decision. When you are planning your business, one of your biggest decisions will be: Where do I locate?

The location of your business can have a major effect upon your success. And it is wise to consider the downside as well as the upside of locating your business in your home.

The Home Handicaps

Most of us would love to work at home. Most of us have nice homes, in nice places, and share them with people we enjoy. Yet working out of your home can add a series of powerful and unnecessary handicaps to your attempts to become a professional member of the successful self-employed. Many of the entrepreneurs we have interviewed started their businesses in their homes. Some still work there. But many eventually decided to set up offices outside their homes.

Before you decide on a home office as your place of business, consider these drawbacks. We list them as possibilities because not all entrepreneurs encounter them. Yet all entrepreneurs should consider them before they make a decision on where to have their office.

The People You Love May Not Be the People You Love to Have Involved in Your Business

An entrepreneur we talked to told us this story: "It was my first day of working at home. I have already sent my first fax and am expecting one in return. My spouse walks in to ask whether I could help by picking up the kids at school. As I look at her, I feel an emotion I never had before. I wish she weren't there. She has, in some way, invaded my territory. By her very presence she seems to compromise my new life, my new idea of myself as a successful entrepreneur, working out of a professional home office."

You may be currently living with a consenting adult you have real affection for. It is a relationship you wish to continue in the future. This is helpful, because as you go out on your own and take on a huge range of new and complicated challenges, the last thing you need is a complicated personal life.

So we heartily congratulate you on a happy home life, and encourage you to do everything possible to keep it that way—by keeping your loved one, and your love life, *separate* from your business life.

We are hopeful that your loved one supports your new venture and is even eager to help. That emotional support will be needed. But we hasten to caution you that we have met few successful couples who live together and work together. We have met a few, and we will introduce them later on; but *most* entrepreneurs find that doing business with someone you love can add a lot of strain to an otherwise loving relationship.

There seems to be something that works against making love and making money with the same individual.

This is not to say that it can't be done—but the odds don't favor a happy consummation of this coupling. And why impose this added burden on yourself? Do you really want to discuss business in bed?

So we strongly recommend you establish some boundaries and keep your business world separate from your love life.

If You Think Kids Can Drive You Nuts—Wait Until They Interrupt a Crucial Business Call

An entrepreneur told us this story: "I was in the midst of a conference call to France. My French is not so good, and their English is . . . imperfect. My two-year-old son chose that moment to enter the room. He was looking for attention. He ran over to me and started to reach for the phone. I politely—but firmly—kept him away. He began to get angry, and there is nothing like the rage of a two-year-old. He started to scream. My French customer said: 'Is there a *baby* in your office?' "

We are sure that, if you've been fortunate enough to have children, you love them dearly. It would be unnatural if you didn't. But it is equally unnatural to expect children to accept the fact that, if you are home, they can't be with you. They will continually be coming in to see you, and enthusiastically interrupting you. They don't mean any harm by this, but it can drive you nuts.

Another entrepreneur put it this way: "I have two teenage kids at home. Within months of opening my office in my home, I realized that it wasn't going to work. They were on the home phone, *and* on my office phone. Teenagers can find a phone—no matter what. Once I had a client who couldn't get through—for hours. He thought I was home, but all he got was a busy signal. He couldn't even leave a message. I decided I could either spend all my time yelling at my teenagers to get off the phone, or find another place to work."

You don't want to spend your time yelling at your kids. You didn't go out on your own so that you could replace all those people who used to drive you crazy at your former company— with your own children. You don't want to make your children your enemies and grow to see them as a problem impeding your progress. They could be. And they could be a more powerful and intrusive problem than any you encountered in the corporate infighting of your previous job. You don't want to get impatient or angry with your own kids. Yet you have work to do. So don't set up your place of business where they can visit you as easily as they can walk into your bedroom.

Hiring Outsiders to Work in Your Home

A basic handicap of a home office is that it is hard to expand. We hope your business needs to expand. If it does, you will need to hire some excellent people. In fact, there's probably never been a better time to hire people. There are seasoned professionals out on the street, eager to help. And young MBAs, desperate for their first job. You can hire great people with high energy who can help you build your business.

But it is hard to bring outsiders home. It's like building a business family and having another family in the same house.

An entrepreneur told us: "I had a major presentation to prepare. There were six of us working on it, for three days—around the clock. My office was in my home—and you can imagine what that did to my family. They still haven't forgiven me for all that disruption."

And if you think a home office can have negative effects *inside* the home, just wait until you see the impression it creates *outside.*

How to Lose Friends and Turn Off Prospects

A successful entrepreneur offering out-sourcing of personnel functions to high-tech companies told us of one of his first experiences of what it was really like to have a home office. A friend of *his* had become CEO of a Silicon Valley company. Immediately he wrote to his friend, who was now also a hot prospect, offering the services of his new company. Within days the friend called. After some friendly pleasantries, he was asked about his new company. "And where is your office?" the potential customer asked him. "At home," the entrepreneur said. "You mean," the prospect said, "your own home. With Alice and the kids? We were thinking of doing business with a larger concern." The conversation ended cheerfully enough, but he knew that he'd lost the chance to get the business.

The lesson: It is very hard for a friend, who knew you when, to think of your home, the one he visited to have fun, as a serious place of business.

We hope you have a lot of friends. They will be an important emotional support group as you head out into the difficult world of the self-employed. Everyone can be a possible business lead. But we have found that your close friends usually don't produce significant business for you. They will be eager to help you. And they will be cheering you on—as we all do to those more adventurous people we know. But don't expect them to produce real business. Don't even ask them to. For real leads from your closest friends are rare. It is more likely to be from an acquaintance. Or—most likely of all—from a professional colleague. Or even a "cold call."

And if you work out of your home, even your good friends will take you less seriously than if you have set up an office somewhere else in a more professional environment.

You can lose your friends if you put them in the awkward position of trying to get business for you. They will be embarrassed by their lack of success, and eventually stop calling.

And your home office doesn't help your friends believe you want to really make it big. After all, they are probably your neighbors. If a neighbor started working out of his home, would you believe that he was going to set the world on fire? Or would you think that he had chosen a comfortable lifestyle rather than an ambitious business plan? Which leads to our next point . . .

You Occupy a Different Place in Your Client's Mind When You Set Up Your Office Outside Your Home

An entrepreneur tells us this compelling story: "Our company was growing internationally. Money was tight, but we needed an office badly. We opened what we called an office in Europe. But the office was actually in the apartment of our European manager. It was a big apartment, and that decision seemed to make sense. We saved on overhead, and our European manager could walk out of his bedroom and begin his day. We didn't think our customers would want to visit our office in Europe. Until a very straightlaced crew from a major company that was our biggest customer showed up. It was a hot summer day, and our employees were dressed . . . casually. In jeans and shorts. Even our manager was wearing an open-necked shirt and a pair of slacks, while the big company people looked like they had come from a board of directors meeting—all pinstripe suits and button-down shirts.

"But the fact that our office was a person's apartment was the single awesome reality that they could not get over. They withdrew their business and told us: 'Call us when you get a real office.' We pleaded with them, we begged them not to withdraw their business—for they were our biggest customer. But it was not until almost a year later, when we were able to physically escort them to a professional-looking office, that we were able to reestablish our relationship."

It might not be rational, but customers don't have to be rational. For whatever reasons, they feel more comfortable in giving business to those who have "real" offices. Offices outside their home. This is particularly true if you are just starting out in business and don't have a long track record to point to. A professional office environment confirms that you have a serious commitment to your business. An office image can then be a deciding factor. As mentioned, later on we will talk about the importance of being a brand. A professional business person works in an office. That is part of the successful brand identity. If you want to be perceived as a successful business person, it is *a lot easier* if you have an address that is different from your home address—even if it's just the building across the street. (Of course, we recognize that not everybody can afford an office outside the home, but we believe it should be one of your first business objectives.)

Yes—You Still Have to Get Dressed in the Morning

Gay Talese is a well-known author who gets up every morning and puts on a jacket and a tie. Has breakfast with his wife, checks the paper. Then he walks out his front door. And around the block. He then pulls out a separate key and opens the door to the apartment in the basement of his building—which is his *office.* By that very act of getting dressed and walking around the block, he has effectively established the essential distance between *home life* and *work life.*

Perhaps you can conduct business in your pajamas—if you happen to wear pajamas. But we feel that it is wise to be dressed as a businessperson when you conduct your business. *As a budding entrepreneur, you will have to make a special effort for people to take you seriously.* And you have to take yourself seriously. People want to do business with others who take their business seriously. If you wander downstairs, in casual attire, to make some important calls, you are putting the odds against delivering the businesslike impression you wish to convey. This doesn't necessarily mean wearing a coat and a tie or a dress, but proper business attire. Clothes you would feel comfortable wearing in a professional environment. Then you will feel more comfortable and confident when you transact your business. We don't know why it works that way—it just does.

Is it a completely irrelevant coincidence that almost every person who makes large sums of money dresses up when they do business? It is a mark of respect for those you intend to do business with.

Do you want people to focus on what you are wearing—or not wearing—or do you want them to hire you for you ideas or buy your product?

Are tribal costumes necessary to be successful in business? We wish they weren't. They are. Even in a home office.

Keeping Regular Hours Will Keep You Ahead

As our list of home handicaps grows, you are probably saying to yourself: "But I thought going out on my own was going to be more fun!"

And we know it probably isn't "fun" to think of getting dressed in professional attire and then having to keep regular hours. After all, you wanted to be more of a free spirit. But customers don't do business with free spirits. They hire practical businesspeople—whatever the business they are in.

Businesspeople whom they can trust to be at their office when they call. And they will call between normal business hours—usually eight-thirty and six. That doesn't mean you will be working regular business hours. You will have to work beyond any hours you ever expected. You will never completely stop working or at least thinking about business again.

But you have to think of the impression you are creating from the customers' point of view. If they call and you are not there, this sets up uncertainty in their minds. Remember: You no longer have the major brand of a big company behind you. Now you have to do everything to reassure your prospects that you can be just as reliable as you were before—only more so. Because now you can really concentrate on their business.

But this idea is only credible if you are accessible. Easily, and regularly accessible. This is no time to take afternoons off. Answering machines don't cut it. Customers want to talk to you—that's why they hired you. You have got to be more sensitive than ever to their concerns for stability and all the other mundane virtues—which were taken for granted when you had a big name branded on your hide.

And regular hours and home life just don't mix. A plumbing emergency will grab your attention. Your spouse needs you to do him a favor—right now. You have to take the kids to the dentist. A thousand and one domestic crises can intrude on your office hours if your office is in your home. And there is no way to resist. After all, are you going to have the almost suicidal courage to be daily demonstrating that your business is more important to you than your home, your loved ones, and your friends?

Discipline Is Harder at Home

One minute you resolve to always be at your desk and working by nine. But the very next minute an old friend calls who is in town for the day and begs you to have a cup of coffee with her. You don't get to see her very often—she lives on the opposite coast—so you agree. By the time you get home from coffee, there is a "tree man" waiting to talk to you. You hadn't realized it, but it seems that all the trees in your yard are in need of attention.

Some are actually a danger to your neighbors—you could be sued if they fell on their houses. Thoroughly upset, you find it hard to begin the job at hand. Then you hear a knocking at your door. There is someone representing a home improvement outfit that would like to give you a free estimate of what it would cost to paint your house. *You realize, with a sinking heart, that your house has become a kind of marketing focus in modern America.* And every salesperson, selling everything from tree and house repair to magazines and Girl Scout cookies, feels free to ring your bell. It is hard to maintain any sense of a disciplined day with this unending series of interruptions. Let alone keep your own *self-discipline* in place.

We have heard many stories like these from entrepreneurs who start out trying to work out of their homes. Discipline is hard in the face of constant, "necessary" interruptions. What did all these people do before there were home offices?

An entrepreneur we met has shared with us these notes from the home front: "When I first tried to work out of my home, my discipline crumbled. It didn't collapse. It wasn't as though one day I threw all caution to the wind and played tennis until I couldn't walk. It was more subtle than that.

"First, it was a tennis game with some new friends Wednesday afternoons. I rationalized this as a perk I granted myself. Being your own boss has its advantages, I told myself.

"Then I found myself going to movies in the afternoon. It was so much nicer than having to wait in line. There was a kind of gleeful luxury to going into a theater, to a hit movie, with so few people in the audience.

"I then started to find museums equally alluring. It was so wonderful to get back to an appreciation for the finer things—and it was only a thirty-minute drive from my home. And avoiding crowds if I went at odd hours. I began to lead a counterclockwise life—doing the things I loved to do during the day, and then working all night.

"I told myself it made sense, until a customer asked me, 'What the hell is going on?' It was more concern than anger. He'd seen me in blue jeans heading into a movie theater at ten o'clock one morning in New York. He was worried that I was failing. Actually, my business was going quite well—but I was living two lives.

"And I realized I had to make a choice. My discipline had crumbled in many small ways until I was leading an unconventional lifestyle that was growing more and more out of control."

They say the road to hell is paved with good intentions. And the home office is full of good intentions that lead to a kind of business hell. For business becomes an interruption in your life. And you yield to temptations—like midweek tennis—while your business life is on the line. Starting a new business takes all the focus and discipline you've got.

It is easier—much easier—to be disciplined in an environment in which everyone around you is working in an organized and disciplined way.

Perhaps you are more organized and more disciplined than most of the entrepreneurs we have talked to. But why test yourself? Why not make it easy to succeed? Leave the temptations at home.

Business Opportunities Don't Happen at Home

Part of the art of the entrepreneurial life is putting yourself in situations in which good things can happen to you. One of your greatest challenges is to make sure you are still at the heart of the business world. You didn't set up your company to become a fringe player—yet there is a kind of centrifugal force. If you are not in the center of the action, you can be gradually pushed to the outer regions, where the business pickings are slimmer. Remember: For the entrepreneur, silence is not golden.

When you get an office, you will be located in a business world.

There will be people doing business all around you. Thus, the odds dramatically increase that you might meet someone who might introduce you to someone who knows someone who could use your services. Having coffee in your kitchen at home is a lousy form of business networking.

The Loneliness of the Long-Distance Worker

It is another day at your home office—located miles away from any fellow workers. You peck away at your computer, but it is hard for you to get motivated. You yearn for someone to talk to. You get a call—a piece of good news. You would love to walk down the hall and tell someone. Anyone. It is human nature to enjoy being part of a team. But you are now a team of one. And you find you miss the sense of other people to talk with, to share your daily battles. You even miss the sense of office *noise*—that constant chirping of faxes and phones that indicates business is being done.

It is natural to feel lonely when you are alone. Which you will be if you are located in your home. No ability to affectionately examine the ruins of the night before with a sympathetic gaggle of friends. No team-sport deadlines, when everyone is rushing together to get something done. No laughter at some foolish boss. You are the boss, and the employee. You miss the feeling of having hardworking people around you.

There is an alternative. Often you will find another entrepreneur who is willing, even eager, to share office space. (One caution: Be sure that you are both clear on who pays for what. An entrepreneur tells us: "I once found myself in a barter situation in which I had agreed to give a certain amount of time in exchange for rent, but the expectations of my real estate partner about what I had to do in exchange for our space were so outlandish we ended up disliking the very thought of sharing space. I learned the hard lesson that my time was valuable, and it was not worth it for me to trade large amounts of it for a small rent.")

Another option becoming more and more popular is to go to a central location, a core group of offices: a *virtual office,* with phones and faxes and probably even a receptionist because the sound of a human voice is still so reassuring. Here, you will be surrounded by fellow entrepreneurs, people just like yourself, fighting the same fight. You will be able to share stories and faxes, computers and conference rooms with them. And help each other fight on another day. There you will find the comradeship you might be missing. It will also give you a chance to avoid becoming a technoholic.

Home Offices Encourage Technoholics

A small-business owner shared this harrowing story: "It happened to me gradually, without my really realizing it. It was lonely at home, with no one from my business to talk to, and gradually I began to spend more and more time with my technical toys.

"I would spend hours, even days, lost on the Net. I would rationalize that I was doing research for some customer.

"I found myself sending electronic mail to people I didn't know, but who were interested in similar subjects. I joined discussions on home improvements and how to buy a great case of French wine. I would use the printer at the slightest provocation.

"And then I became convinced that everything in my life would work better if I could just purchase a more powerful, more exciting model of my computer. I began to fantasize about owning the ultimate computer. A computer that could allow me to edit films . . . although editing films had absolutely nothing to do with my basic business. Finally I came to see that I had become a *technoholic*—trying to use technology to take the place of all those fellow workers. Having a home office is dangerous for any potential technoholic. It is like drinking alone. Once you start, you are on the downward, obsessive path."

If you see signs in yourself that you are becoming a technoholic try these tricks: limit yourself to a specific time on the Net. Use faxes and phones—only when absolutely necessary. And resist buying the next, hottest computer. Recognize that by being a technoholic you can jeopardize your home life.

It's Easier than Ever to Have an Office Outside Your Home

You are about to become a real estate expert. In setting up your own business, you quickly discover the importance of that famous litany: location, location, location. You will not believe how many elevators you will go up, how many corridors you will walk down. But be relieved: It is a buyers' market.

These days, in many parts of the country, it is easy to set up a professional office environment. You can even have your phone answered for a minimal charge. This does not mean that you'll have to invest a huge sum in a long lease or add conspicuously to your overhead. Just take a small, simple office. It can even be a cubicle with a phone and a desk upon which you can rest your portable computer. Even if it is five minutes from your home. The vital trick is to put some *distance* between your personal life, which you still would like to have, and your business life, which will eat up all your time unless you are careful.

Psychological and Physical Separation Is the Key in Creating a Productive Office—and a Happy Home

Some new entrepreneurs find that they must work out of their home. If you *must,* then it is crucial to set up a clear separation. You need walls . . . a place to go and be a worker bee. Role-playing is part of life. And you must learn to shift from roommate or lover or mom or husband to professional. Any psychological or physical distance you set up will help you in this pursuit.

While it is easier than ever to go out and find an office, it is also possible to create an office space in your home. As long as you set the proper goal: not *integration* with your home life, but *separation* from it. Separate phone lines, fax lines, all your tools to connect you to the larger business world must be distinct from those lifelines to friends and family.

A friend of ours set up what she calls "My Berlin Wall." It is a simple divider between her kitchen and her dining room. When it is up, her family knows that she is at work and cannot be disturbed. This is a convertible wall and can come down when the family wishes to entertain.

One entrepreneur now in her own office told us why she left home. She had tried to set up an office in her apartment—which she shared with a roommate who had a traditional day job in an office building. Since her roommate was gone during the day, our intrepid entrepreneur decided to set up a *convertible* office in their New York apartment. In the day the living room was an office; at night the desk was folded up, the computer stashed away, and it became an apartment living space once more. Of course, this kind of arrangement can lead to problems. For example, one day her roommate was sick. She had to ask her sick roommate to hide in the bedroom all day. It would have ruined the office atmosphere if a client coming there for a meeting had seen her sick roommate parading around in her pajamas. Which leads to our final point . . .

Keep Your House a Home and Your Office . . . an Office

Your house is meant to be a home. A "shelter from the stormy blast." Your "castle" where you can go and pull up the drawbridge, let your hair down, and find a cozy fire burning, with loved ones to nurture you when the barbarian world doesn't seem to care. Your house can be a place of regeneration and inspiration. It can give you the strength to fight on another day. Let your house be a loving home. That is what your house does best.

And then your office can do what it does best: act as an arena for your focused business energies. It can be your happy hunting ground, where you go, properly dressed for the business fray, and love to hear the phones ringing and the faxes faxing all day long.

When you first go out and set up your business, it is your chance to introduce yourself to a whole range of people. They will respect you more, and you will function better, if you have an office location that is different from where you live.

If this different location is not possible at the beginning, you should, as we have discussed, make an extra, conscious effort to establish that vital *separation* between home life and work life. Separate doors help. Different rules, such as "Mommy cannot be disturbed when she is in her office." Different phone lines. The more physical and psychological distance between your office and your living quarters, the better.

Then your house can be what it should be ... *a welcome home.*

Now that we've discussed *where* you should work, it is time to decide *who* you should work with. Which is the subject of our next two chapters.

Fired Up! Fired Up! Fired Up! Fired Up! Fired Up! Fired Up! Fired Up! Fired Up! Fired Up! Fired Up! Fired Up! Fired Up!

62

Partnership Without the Joy of Sex

"Your partner should have different strengths than you have, but you should share the same values."

—*Bill Backer, creator, with his partner Carl Spielvogel, of one of the most successful advertising agencies in America*

Many people, upon leaving a big corporation for the cold world outside, feel it will be a lot warmer if they can get together with a good partner. And there are many examples of successful partnerships—entrepreneurs who worked positively together to build a profitable business.

But there are also many instances when a partnership didn't work. Many businesses fail due to fallouts between partners. Therefore, it is essential that if you are choosing a partner, you find the right one.

Based on our research of successful entrepreneurial partnerships, we have concluded that the most effective partnerships are founded on a fundamental idea: *Work with someone who has opposite strengths but similar values.* Out of this fundamental underlying principle flow many other specific partnership principles.

Partnerships that don't follow this fundamental principle—of dissimilar strengths and similar values—are doomed to failure.

In this chapter you will read about successful partnerships

and unsuccessful ones. You will discover that there are alternatives to having a partner that can still bring you the support you might feel you need.

We have also prepared a simple series of partnership trials that will allow you to have experiences with your possible partner that will help you to determine if he or she is the right partner for you.

It is worth devoting a great deal of time and thought to selecting the right partner, for the wrong partner can permanently affect your business. We have learned of many cases where otherwise effective entrepreneurs were forced into early failure through choosing a partner who turned out to be a pernicious influence. Such an occurrence is more common than you might believe. And such imploding partnerships can ruin all chances for success for both the people involved.

We hope you *never* have to go through an experience a friend of ours had when she was on a plane to Chicago to sign the single biggest business deal she'd ever made—and her *partner* turned to her and said, "I want out of this. I want a divorce from our deal. I hate you."

Somehow, she was able to calm her partner down, and they got the deal done. And the partnership was over. But the point of the story is that a partnership—good or bad—will probably be a new experience for you, especially if you have spent most of your life in the more balanced and organized team-sport atmosphere of a large corporation.

A partnership is not a team sport. It is two or more people adrift in a raft, each with a large oar and often no land in sight, with a bad storm blowing and the waves rising. There are no corporate captains to settle disputes on your partnership raft— you have to duke it out together.

A partnership can be the most intense and most frustrating relationship you've ever had. It can be the most enjoyable and productive. It can also be the most dangerous.

When you are out there trying desperately to survive, and it's just you and your partner confronting all the crises that will occur, you had better be sure you picked the *right* person to share your business life with.

You might even discover that you are not the type of person who needs or should have a partner. Having a lifelong business partner is no longer a necessity. In fact, there are many nontraditional types of partnerships that work extremely well in the entrepreneurial world of today. So it is ideal to take your time and review your options.

To help you in that crucial endeavor, we now discuss, with some specific illustrations, some *proven* principles—developed through our own experience and the experience of hundreds of successful entrepreneurs we have studied—to use when selecting a possible partner. These principles apply whether you are thinking of setting up a retail store, building a consulting firm, or creating a major manufacturing capability. We call these our *Partnership Principles.* Tack them up on the wall of your office to remind yourself of what you are getting into. You can use these Partnership Principles as an invaluable checklist for you to go through *before* you decide to team up with anybody.

Partnership Principles

Opposites Attract Because They Work

In business life, as well as romantic love, opposites can attract. There seems to be a functional magnetism at the heart of the universe that encourages diverse types to come together. The wave seeks the shore, the sun balances the moon, everyone has a need for *something* more. Something more, and usually something *different,* is what your partner can bring to your venture.

If you have exactly the same strengths, one of you is probably not essential.

You need a partner who can be strong where you are weak. If you are creative but disorganized, she should be logical and organized. If you are methodical and conscientious, he should be exciting and risk-taking.

Even physical differences can combine into an attractive unity—one partner being young and beautiful, one being older and more "experienced."

Male—female. Large and small. Intellectual—emotional.

As two eyes make one in sight, so two points of view are helpful in determining the best course to take in business.

Yet it is also *crucial to make sure that while you may have very different appearances, backgrounds, and strengths, you share the same values.*

One of the entrepreneurs we talked to made the mistake of starting her business with a partner who wanted to get rich quick and retire to Tahiti. While our friend also wanted to make money, her goal was not to cash out as quickly as possible, but rather, *on the contrary,* to build a long-running and successful business with clients she enjoyed. In other words, her values and goals were very different. And she found herself at key points in her relationship yelling at her financially ambitious partner because they had such different aspirations. All this could have been determined, and settled, far in advance of her launch.

Complementary and *different* strengths, yet *similar* values is the ideal, if paradoxical combination, in a partner.

A good example of opposites that worked together well is the story of two friends of ours: Carl Spielvogel and Bill Backer. They worked at a large advertising agency together and decided to go out on their own. As two opposite kinds of people, when they became partners, their very differences provided the right balance for success.

Bill Backer says, "Most of our friends in advertising told us our partnership wouldn't last more than a few months. It lasted for fifteen years, while we built the agency into one of the best in America."

Bill Backer was what is known in advertising as a "creative" person. He created the famous commercial "I want to buy the world a Coke."

He also helped create the "Tastes great, less filling" advertising that turned Miller Lite into a best-selling beer. Because of his outstanding creativity, Bill has been elected to the Advertising Hall of Fame.

"When it comes to making a decision one of the partners has to be in charge," Bill says. "Carl was in charge of all the financial and business matters. I consulted with Carl on any major advertising campaign, but, ultimately, I was in charge of the creative."

Carl Spielvogel was a very organized "account" person, who had an amazing gift for staying in touch with a great many people—especially clients. He was a superlative *networker*. A former college roommate of his, whom Carl always stayed in close touch with, became head of Philip Morris, the company that bought Miller, which became Carl and Bill's biggest client.

With Carl's connections, and Bill's creative ability, they built Backer & Spielvogel, one of the fastest-growing advertising agencies of that time.

Carl provided the business sense and client service, Bill provided the creative magic. Carl wrote many notes to clients, while Bill wrote many songs.

They made many millions for themselves, and their clients.

Carl is an extroverted and gregarious man, a former reporter for *The New York Times*, who was happy to give his great energy to his community, becoming a member of the board of trustees of the Metropolitan Museum of Art, one of the highest-profile roles in the exciting artistic and social life of the Big Apple.

Bill is a cultivated southern gentleman who prefers weekends on his beautiful Virginia estate.

Carl is a man of clipped sentences and positive, energetic action.

Bill is a friendly, relaxed fellow, who loves to tell a story and values people who are "kind and talented."

Their different temperaments and interests created a well-balanced environment that encouraged productive and effective work.

Either one, on his own, might have been too extreme. Together, they occupied a powerful center. The very fact that they were different added immeasurably to their strength.

They did not spend a lot of time together after hours. Another strength. For knowledge of different worlds helped them to see challenges with better, more far-reaching perspectives.

Bill describes the success of their partnership this way: "You should share a sense of taste, and approach to life. In general, you should agree on what in the world you consider good, and what you believe is a good outcome to your combined efforts.

"You should share values in terms of the kind of people you want to work with. Both Carl and I wanted to work with talented people, who were also honest and enjoyable to work with. This was an important value in building our business.

"Carl and I were opposites in many skill areas, and were a good balance for each other. But in the area of fundamental values, the way we conducted the business, we were united. That was the secret of our success, and of the success of our partnership."

Opposite strengths yet shared values work together to build successful partnerships.

The reverse, then, as you would expect, is often true: Watch out when two *too similar* types get together.

Similar Types Can Sink Each Other

Two entrepreneurs we talked to had a lot in common. In fact, it turned out *they had too much in common to build a successful business.*

They had both worked at successful art galleries in Manhattan. They both decided they would like to have an art gallery of their own. They discussed the plans over coffee in SoHo. They were excited by each other's enthusiasm. They were both creative, high-strung, attractive people—who loved to party. Neither one had enjoyed math in high school. Both were rather vague about details. Details like dates and times. Their friends found their continual lateness amusing; later their artists did not. And since they were so similar in style, there was no one to complain to.

They got an immediate, positive reaction to their new gallery. They opened with a show in which several talented artists were represented. The media, whom they knew, were kind, even enthusiastic.

A year later they hated each other. She thought he had blown it. He thought she had blown it. The truth was, they had blown it together. By teaming up with a mirror image of themselves, they reinforced the best and worst qualities. The best qualities helped them soar and gain early success, but their worst qualities caused them to fail equally rapidly. Neither one of them chose to spend any time on the business side of the business, and an art gallery is, in the end, a business. Neither one wanted to look after all the mundane yet essential details, the hundreds of appointments and specifics that it takes to organize a big show. Neither one of them wanted to have lengthy, supportive conversations with the artists. Together, they were an impossible combination, like hearing a constant echo of a single note, rather than a beguiling harmony.

In a partner, choose someone who can complement your weaknesses with his strengths.

The essential paradox: Opposites attract because they work.

Your partner should balance your weakness with her strengths, just as you can balance her weakness with your strengths. It is like a successful marriage. In fact, some partnerships *are* marriages.

Marriage Partnerships—with the Right Balance—Can Work in Business

John Gray, the owner of Bubbies Pickles, whom we discussed earlier, was first thinking of leaving his job as vice president of a major bank in San Francisco when he fell in love with Kathy, who was also an officer at the bank.

Her specialty was operations. His was marketing. Opposites attract, and they fell in love.

Ten years after they got married, they bought a pickle company in Stockton. It was natural that John should concentrate on marketing and that Kathy should be in charge of operations. And that is the way it has worked out.

Today, their successful venture is run just as they had begun: John handles the key distribution and marketing challenges; Kathy makes sure that the whole operation works as efficiently and productively as possible.

Once again, their diverse strengths balance each other in a successful way. And when you add the power of shared values, you have an unbeatable combination.

Trust Built on Shared Values Can Be a Business Asset

"The wonderful thing," John says, "is that you don't have to worry about your business partners' commitment when you are married. You can really trust each other because you both have so much to lose. You are not only betting on the success of a business—but of a whole life together.

"Kathy and I have sat up many nights planning the future of the business. It is exciting to have someone who is so in touch with the same issues, and you can be free to discuss everything openly. In addition, the decisions made together seem better than ones we make alone. Just talking something over with someone you are so close to and who knows you and the business so well can really give you confidence that you will come out with a good direction. And then, when you go to implement the idea, you don't have to worry about getting support.

"In corporate situations, you often have to shade the truth, or encounter opposition because of internal politics. You certainly can't trust everyone else or your corporate peers to have the same degree of concern in the success of an idea as you do. When you are married, and married to the business, you have twice the trust, the power, and the focus."

John and Kathy have been successful in combining different strengths in a successful marriage and a successful business venture because their diverse skills come together in shared values.

And they are not alone. Other couples find that working together is the best of all worlds.

Jean-Paul and Eva Blachere are another example of a married couple who also have built a business together. Coming from Europe to live in America, it was natural for them to tie the two continents together with a great business idea. Once again, it was a partnership based on a set of opposite skills: Jean-Paul handles the marketing and Eva manages the operational aspects of their business.

They have built a successful entrepreneurial operation by importing first-rate quality china and cutlery from France and selling it in America. Their business allows, even demands, that they spend time in both countries. Instead of one or the other having to disappear for weeks or months on lonely business trips, they are able to go together and share their lives in a way that is uniquely enjoyable.

"We love going to France together," Eva Blachere says, "and we love coming back to America. We have a wonderful life—together."

Building a business with the one you love can have many advantages—if you have complementary yet different skills, and temperaments that can make the transition from bedroom to boardroom. Most importantly, you should share both professional and personal values.

For many couples, it can be a disaster to try to turn their married relationship into a business partnership as well. Marriage itself is not a guarantee of a successful entrepreneurial venture. Still, it is true that if you have a good partnership in your marriage, the odds increase that you can have a good business experience.

But one thing is certainly true: Where two can tango, three almost always fail.

In business, as in dancing, beware the ménage à trois. In our study of successful entrepreneurial partnerships, few remain successful when they are joined by a third person. A couple works; a triangle does not.

This is especially true if you introduce your spouse into an already established business partnership.

Ménage à Trois Can Tear a Partnership Apart

Betty and Dorothy were drawn to the health food business. They both loved to cook, and especially loved to cook what they considered healthy food. And they lived in Atlanta—where talking about the latest health food fads had lately become a passionate way of life.

They decided to open a health food store—but a health food store with a difference. Their health food store would be a fun place to be. They would prepare sandwiches and delicious salads, and try to create an atmosphere of a country kitchen.

"We looked upon it," Betty said, "as doing something we loved to do—together."

They started with a small lease for a little store in Peachtree Plaza. Soon the business grew. People came in early, for coffee and "healthy" bagels, and many were there when Betty and Dorothy shut up shop at seven o'clock. They started to offer a catering business—and that was a breakthrough. Suddenly their healthy catering service was the one to have in Atlanta. Every big company wanted them to cater to business gatherings.

As the business grew, it attracted the attention of Dorothy's husband.

Dorothy's husband, Gary, was a commercial artist. Which meant that he often had some time on his hands. Even a successful artist often has time between projects. And even a successful commercial artist is often anxious about his future. It was natural that Gary was attracted to the successful business Betty and his wife Dorothy had created.

Gary began to spend more and more time at the health food store and he became more and more interested in the catering business. First he would just drop in to talk. Then he gradually began to make a habit of stopping by each afternoon and helping Dorothy with different tasks. One day he would help out with menus, another day he would answer the phone.

He seemed to spend more and more time at Dorothy and Betty's operation. It was a busy, cheerful place. They were making money, and yet serving a great many interesting people. Their customers included a healthy number of leading businesspeople and politicians, people who were leaders in the artistic and social life of Atlanta.

It was no wonder that Gary found the atmosphere irresistible. It was so much more enjoyable for him to be part of this energetic and profitable enterprise than sitting at home confronting another blank page.

At first Betty didn't mind Gary's increased involvement. There was lots to do, they were growing so fast, and she thought he could be helpful. But as his presence increased, his manner took on a more and more authoritative tone. Which Betty found outrageous. She and Dorothy had built the business; Gary had had nothing to do with it. Betty had invested her own money, as had Dorothy. Betty knew for a fact that Gary had invested nothing.

But now he seemed to be giving orders. Betty came in one day and saw him sitting at her desk. He told her to run down to the post office and pick up a consignment of new herbs they had ordered.

Betty lost it. She simply blew up at him.

Later, in thinking it over, Betty realized that she was so upset because it had become clear to her that Gary was attempting to take over the business she and Dorothy had started together.

It had become so successful that Gary had decided he wanted a piece of it; and Dorothy, for the sake of her marriage, had obviously gone along.

Betty came to understand, with a great sense of loss, that she could not fight such a powerful combination. The business had been her baby, but now she had to give it up to a third party who wasn't even involved in the conception.

Once Betty understood her losing position in this unworkable ménage à trois, she left the business she had worked so hard to build. She regards her experience as a "professional and personal tragedy. I don't know if I could have seen it coming, but three people is one too many partners, especially when two of them are married. I know that now—for sure."

Don't Expect to Change Your Partner's Values

Wise parents tell their children: "Don't expect to change the person you marry."

To us, this is the most essential idea you must carry with you during your search for a business partner. *Don't expect to change your business partner's basic values.* Just as your partner should not expect to change *you!* You are not kids (not that the character of any child is easy to mold!), and your personality traits and work habits and strengths and weaknesses are long set.

So accept that what you see in a prospective partner is what you will get.

An entrepreneur told us that she had a partner who had an almost pathological need to say yes. No matter what the situation, he couldn't say no. He put a high value on being liked, and he hated to say no.

His propensity for saying yes when no would have been more appropriate kept getting the partnership into trouble. There were many disappointed customers because the business simply couldn't fulfill his optimistic promises.

She spent many fruitless hours trying to get her partner to be more reasonable about promising customers impossible achievements. "At first I thought he would learn because he made us look so terrible. But then I realized that he was never going to change. He just couldn't say no, and he wasn't about to start for me or any other partner. Being reasonable was just not in his character.

"Yet he had many other business strengths. He was intelligent and energetic. I just should never have expected him to change."

Since people don't change, it is wise to make sure you are clear on your roles and your basic values—before you become partners.

And if it is true that it is hard to change the values of your partner when you share the same country and culture, it is definitely impossible to change his values when he comes from another country and business context.

When Cultural Values Clash

An entrepreneur building a major business operation in Europe ended up with a powerful Swedish partner. He was pleased—at first. Sweden had always seemed to him to be an attractive country. Didn't they make Saabs? And Volvos?

He also liked the fact that his Swedish partner spoke English and numerous other languages. He looked forward to working with his partner to build his business throughout Europe.

Unfortunately, he had overlooked significant cultural value differences—especially when it came to business values.

One example: His Swedish partner did not believe in the need for elaborate written contracts. While theoretically in complete agreement with his partner, our American friend was well aware that you could get into deep trouble if you tried to do business without spelling out exactly what you intended to do.

But his Swedish partner went ahead and negotiated several agreements based on little more than a handshake.

The Swede assured him that he could trust Europeans. The Swede was proceeding from the values he had learned in his native business climate. "We are not like you Americans," he said. "We do not live by contracts. We don't put our value on paper. We value a man's word."

Today, our American friend and his Swedish partner are out of business.

Yet his Swedish partner refuses to face the reality that the world does not share the business values of a trustful country like Sweden. Or the reality of the more "buyer beware" confrontational business culture of America. The world is full of diverse cultures that behave in their own ways.

Conclusion: Having a partner from a different culture can significantly complicate your relationship—especially when it comes to agreeing on core values in how you conduct your business. And it is wise, indeed essential, to discuss your values and your ideas about how to conduct the business—ahead of time.

Ahead of time is also the right time to make sure you determine your roles.

Discuss Roles—Ahead of Time

Once you get to know each other and have decided that you have different yet complementary strengths and shared values, and that you might want to go into business together, it is a good idea to discuss your roles with your prospective partner. Who will be the new expert at cold calls? Who will write the proposals? Who will manage the personnel issues? Who is a naturally good administrator? What are you financial needs and expectations? Is your partner willing to travel or relocate if the business demands it? Are you?

Do you both *agree* on where you'd like to go in the business?

This discussion can be held well before you get in business to-gether, when there is less risk if you discover that you have very different priorities.

An entrepreneur we talked with launched a successful inter-national consulting firm. She had major clients sign up. She took on a partner. Together they were even more successful. But it turned out that to really deliver on the opportunities, at least one of them would have to live in Eastern Europe. It became im-possible to be solely U.S.-based.

But neither partner wanted to make the personal commitment that living in Eastern Europe would represent. Each was willing to travel there—when necessary. They would even be willing to live there for weeks or months at a time. But neither partner was willing to set up life outside America.

So they had to bring on additional partners who were already based in Eastern Europe and could more easily oversee the busi-ness there. But by taking on those extra partners, they lost a chance for greater profits and greater control.

Moving to Eastern Europe was a subject that could have easily been discussed before they set up their business. As it was, they were lucky to end up with any business at all.

So get your roles clear before you begin working together. To make such decisions after the fact can be costly—even fatal.

Make Sure Your Partner Has as Much to Lose as You do—or You Won't Be Able to Win

A now successful entrepreneur discovered—too late—that one of the people who became his partner could afford to lose. Don't go in business with someone who thinks he or she can *afford to lose.* It makes losing that much more likely.

His partner was just too rich. Yes, it can happen. Money—

large sums of money—can take the edge off an ambitious person. This partner had been given several million dollars as part of a divorce settlement. After experiencing several professional reversals that are—as we have said—an integral part of entrepreneurial life when you are trying to build a new business, she started to take her job less seriously and her travel plans more seriously. She took a trip around the world and then became involved in buying a new apartment. In other words, her personal life took on much more importance than her business life once she realized that it wasn't uninterrupted fun to be an entrepreneur. She had expected it to be much more glamorous than it really was. She left, and it took her partner a year to build the forward momentum she had disrupted by her sudden departure.

This story illustrates the fact that it is important to discuss in specific detail what your professional commitment will be today and what your expectations are for the future. It is also essential to be honest about your financial needs or lack of financial ambition. If one partner is less interested in making money, he or she will probably also be less interested in putting in the hard work that is necessary in any new business.

Problems arise from the fact that the fear of failing is not equally shared. At three o'clock in the morning, one partner can be home in bed and one can be in the office knocking his brains out. It isn't fair, and it makes for an angry partnership. An unequal division of labor, reflecting a difference in ambition that translates into how hard you are willing to work to build a business, can sink a partnership.

Partners should contribute an equal amount of time to their business. Nothing is more destructive to a partnership than for one partner to feel that he or she is being taken advantage of.

The best rule in partnerships is fifty-fifty—both partners contribute equally in terms of money, skills, dedication, and time.

For partners are not bosses or employees. The very word *partner* conjures up a similar sharing of the risks and a shared passion about the business.

You can't work with people unless you believe they are *equally* involved. And starting a new business requires one hundred and fifty percent commitment. Your partners have to care just as much as you do. And show it with their behavior. Anything less just won't work.

Can You Trust Your Partner with Your Life?

Although you think of yourself as simply starting a business, you should realize that your success or failure in this venture can affect *all* aspects of your life. So don't get in business with someone you can't trust. Trust is an emotion that comes when you instinctively know that you share similar values.

Our emphasis on this emotion comes because, once again, we believe your feelings can give you a good indication of whether you and your partner share the same values. Without this emotional trust, it is wise not to go forward. A lot of partnerships—like a lot of marriages—end up in court.

And there is no foolproof way to judge whether your prospective partner, if tempted by better offers or just pure mercenary greed, won't betray you. But at least you should *start* your relationship *convinced* of his professional and personal integrity.

Here, as in many entrepreneurial decisions, it is wise to go with your instincts. Listen, as we have suggested earlier, to your "intelligent emotions." If you have any instinctive negative vibrations about a future partner, it is wise to stop.

Trust is essential. When your partner is not there, you will want to believe that she is acting in your interest.

There is no way you can watch your partner every minute of

every day. The best partners have a trust that clears up all mis-understandings.

Real trust, of course, is a rare emotion. You might be asking yourself at this point if it is necessary to have a partner. If so, we've got some good news for you . . .

Partners Are Not Essential

Some people believe strongly in being in business together. Others go at it alone. *Both* can be successful.

Before you decide that you can't survive without a partner, explore the alternatives.

Today, many people are creating what are known as "alliances." These are similar to the concept of parallel computing, when many small computers can be as effective, even more effective, than one huge mainframe. In fact, parallel partnerships have worked in law firms for many generations. They have partners who specialize in tax law, partners who are authorities on setting up trusts, partners who are widely regarded as authorities in corporate takeover battles.

These parallel partners work along their individual lines of interest but form an alliance to share basic resources, such as office space, administrative expenses, and often a pool of junior, hardworking lawyers.

You can form a series of strategic and productive alliances with people who have different specialties. You can share office space with them and all the administrative overhead.

Alliances give you the flexibility to have the right "partner" for the right situation, without locking you into a relationship that might not be perfect for every job. Yet it gives you the importance of continuity and increased stability.

There is also a new variation of the long-standing alliances of parallel partnerships. Today, with the miracles of modern technology (which are, indeed miracles in the life of the successful entrepreneur), you can have what we term . . .

Just-in-Time Partners

Just-in-time partners are those key people whose professional skill in a particular specialty is well known to you. You partner with them as the occasion demands. That is the crucial new dimension to these partnerships. Just-in-time partners are not people you necessarily have to spend the rest of your life with. On the contrary, they are partners for a finite amount of time usually dedicated to a finite objective.

And because they are brought together for just a specific goal, they can be incredibly productive.

It is like gathering an all-star team for a particular business Olympics—you could never afford to have them permanently on staff, but it lets you play in the big leagues when you need to.

An entrepreneur we interviewed was given the opportunity to launch a new product for a major international company. It was an opportunity he didn't want to miss. Yet such a launch would require a range of professional resources he didn't command. He needed people who were expert in marketing, others who could create powerful TV commercials, others who could buy media, and others who understood how to distribute such products.

By forming a series of just-in-time partnerships, he was able to put together an organization that successfully launched the new product.

It was as though he had created a virtual company for a specific time period to launch that particular product. And it was a great company because it consisted entirely of proven, experienced, first-rate people, each expert in his particular field. He had assembled a dream team, and they delivered for him when he needed them.

There are other times in your business life when you might not need an official, legal partner or even a just-in-time partner for a specific opportunity, but you do need someone to talk with. You need what we call an honorary partner, a partnership pal.

Partnership Pals

Partnership pals are often those you have probably known in your previous life—before you became a successful entrepreneur. They became your trusted friends before they had anything to gain. They are not lawyers, doctors, or experts in an area of need—at least in their official role with you. They are pals, trusted pals you can discuss your business with. A pal without agendas, without a desire to work with you or get work from you.

A rare but essential pal indeed.

For just as Sherlock Holmes found great relief in talking over his toughest mysteries with the good Watson, you will want to create a Watson or two of your own to share the mysteries of your entrepreneurial life.

There is nothing better in trying to come to terms with a difficult judgment area than being able to bounce your idea off a friend who can be objective. Just by talking with such an objective audience you can sometimes see options you never even considered. And it is also wise to have someone outside your partnership who can act as your private referee. He can help you decide: "Am I crazy or is the other guy?"

Marilyn Burns, who has built a successful entrepreneurial venture focusing on the educational area, says: "I couldn't have made it without my partnership pals. These were my unofficial board of directors, the people I could reach out to when I had tough decisions to make. I knew I could count on these honorary partners to give me the best advice—without trying to advance their own agendas.

"I have never had a partner," Marilyn says, "but I have always had people I could share my business challenges with."

Sharing business challenges is one of the greatest strengths of any partnership. Now, you still might be thinking to yourself: "But I *do* want to have a partner." If you do, it is time for you to learn how to select one.

How to Select the Right Partner

Selecting the right partner is a thoughtful process. Few of us are fortunate enough to have a chance to try working with our partner before we go into business together.

Tom Margittai, who owned and ran the famous Four Seasons Restaurant in New York, says: "I had trepidations going out on my own. I was forty-four. I knew there were many things I didn't know. I had done well in a big corporation, and in a corporation you could depend on staff services, engineering, legal help, and general staff support. On your own, I knew there would be none of that.

"So I knew I wanted a partner to share the challenge of having a business. *And I decided to select him—rather than just take a chance on someone.*

"I had a partner for over twenty-three years. It was a successful partnership because I had a chance to pick someone I knew well.

"I worked with him for some time *before* we left to set up our business. I was a manager at a large company, and he was my assistant manager. I was impressed with him. I thought he was scrupulously honest.

"I also knew that I was smarter in business matters, and he

was more experienced in restaurant matters like food and wine. It is devastating to have partners with the same kind of talents and the same kind of shortcomings. We were a good balance for each other.

"It would have been a lot harder to do it all on my own," Tom says. "A good partner has made a big, positive difference."

How do *you* select a good partner? You probably won't, as Tom did, have a chance to actually work with him or her in your current business situation.

So how do you select the right person?

We have developed a simple, quick series of trials that you can do—even before you open your own business. They are not infallible. They are no guarantee of partner peace and happiness forevermore. But they are trials we have tested, and they have worked.

We would certainly recommend you try them—before you decide to have a partner. They are so fast and simple, it should appeal to the entrepreneur in you.

Get to Know Your Partner with a Simple Series of Trials—Starting with Breakfast

While there is no real way of discovering what someone might be like when you are risking your business lives together, you can get significant signals—signals that, if you pay attention to your instincts—can help you to figure out what someone might be like as your partner.

One important proviso: You must expect that you will be wanting your prospective partner to win this test. You would only be putting someone to such a series of trials if you were serious about him. And since you are serious about him, you are already looking for proof that he will make a good partner. So be careful not to let your "rational" need for a particular person overwhelm what might be subjective vibrations that say "It's just no go."

With that single proviso, this experience should work well for you.

The first trial is the *breakfast trial.* Invite her to an early breakfast. Seven A.M. Tell her you wish to discuss a business venture with her. Twenty-four hours before, call her and ask if she could possibly get some information on a particular aspect of the venture you are considering. Tell her you have already done some research on it but have some questions about a particular area.

See what she shows up with the next morning. First, see if she shows up on time. Being late to your first breakfast is a bad sign. If she shows up on time and has done the task you asked her, she has almost passed the breakfast test.

But the *key* question in this breakfast trial is: Has she done the task in a way that added something you might have left out? Has she approached the whole challenge in a different way than you would ever have thought of? Here you will find out whether you have *opposite—yet complementary*—skills.

And then ask yourself before the meal is over: Do I really *enjoy* being with this partner? In business, there is a direct correlation between working with someone you enjoy and coming up with effective solutions. Can you create great business ideas together? Is the chemistry good? If you can enjoy someone at breakfast, those late-night crises you will inevitably have will be easier to take.

Next Comes the Party Trial—Where You Find Out if You Really Share the Same Values

Invite him over for a party with some of your friends. This is *not* to see if they like him. You've already determined that you can get along with him, and that's all that matters. But your friends will have impressions that will be helpful to you. They might even bring up things you hadn't noticed. "He seems insecure" is a comment to listen to. Or "He only talks about himself." These are not comments that will determine whether or not you go with your prospective partner, but they *will* help you to understand his weaknesses as well as his strengths.

As part of the party test, you will also discover if your prospective partner has a drinking or smoking habit that might be hard to take in a professional business environment.

One entrepreneur told us, "Today, smoking is really a disruptive habit. Aside from the health issues, if you have a partner who smokes, you are going to have to juggle his needs against the desires of the rest of the staff. And a partner who drinks to excess can't be counted on to deliver." While heavy smoking and drinking might not be illegal, we would advise you to avoid them in a partner.

But the most important part of the party trial is the informal time you will have together. You will be in a relaxed atmosphere in which you can ask him open-ended questions about what he really wants out of life. Listen to his history—it is always a revelation to hear someone describe his life.

You determined in the breakfast trial that you had opposite yet complementary strengths. Now, during an informal evening of various activities and situations, you will have the time you need to really determine whether or not you share the same values.

The Written Trial Comes Next—and It Can Be Revealing

After the party is over, give him a call in a few days. Say that you have been going over all the ideas and you think it would be a good idea if you both, simultaneously yet separately, wrote down exactly what you expected out of the venture and exactly what roles you desired.

Your expectations should be spelled out in black and white.

And this effort can be revelatory. Often, verbalizations are vague. Written plans can reveal major differences.

If—when you share your separate, written plans—they are congruent, congratulations. You have almost found your perfect partner.

But there is one more trial that is essential.

Try to See How You Do—Together

The *cold-call trial is next.* Take your prospective partner to meet a prospect that she has never met. See how well she does, and how well you do *together.* This is a crucial experience, for you've got to be a powerful *combination*—more effective than either one alone. Ask yourself after this meeting whether you would have been better off without her. If the answer is yes, find another partner.

One entrepreneur we talked to almost made a terrible mistake. He didn't realize that a prospective partner of his was a "control freak" until they got into a meeting with a customer. "The guy went nuts. He took total control—and wouldn't let me say anything. Even if you attempt to define areas of control with someone like that, they can't help themselves. 'Control freaks' make the worst partners—usually they destroy the partnership so that they can be in complete control."

A cold-call trial can help you discover whether your partner is a secret control freak or whether, on the other hand, you work well together.

All these trials will give you a better *knowledge* of your prospective partner. You will discover that she is good at certain things and not so good in other areas. This is normal. It is the combination of *both* your qualities that should win you business.

Once you have made the move and selected a partner who balances your strengths and shares your values, hang on as long as you can. Like marriage, it is even more costly to break up a partnership than it is to try to work things through. Once you and your partner are together, it is in your interest, despite all provocations, to keep the partnership going as long as you can.

Many of the challenges encountered early in many entrepreneurships involve mixups about roles, and that can be avoided if you consider the Partnership Principles we have now shared with you. We hope that they will help you to form a more positive business relationship.

Speaking of important relationships, may we introduce you to the elemental threesome of every successful entrepreneur: a great banker, lawyer, and accountant. Yes, they do exist, and in the next chapter we discuss how to find them.

When Your Accountant Becomes Your Best Friend and Lawyers and Bankers Can Be Your Biggest Enemies

"Even if you make a lot of money, you can still be put out of business if you don't understand how to manage your money, and those who handle it for you."

> —*Jeffrey Sellon, who recently sold his company, which had grown to over twenty-five times its original size in less than fifteen years*

When you move from employee to entrepreneur, you are going to have to learn how to *manage your money* in a way you never have before. If cash flow and collecting receivables are not second nature to you, you're in for the learning experience of your life.

And, inevitably, as you enter this new world of financial responsibility, you are going to have to learn how to build *productive relationships* with bankers, lawyers, and your accountant. For without such a team, it will be hard—if not impossible—to actually make any money.

For those of us who have spent our careers working for major companies, collecting money and the complexity of how the company actually got paid was something that other people had to worry about. There was a whole floor or two of accountants.

The Enduring Beauty of a Paycheck

After you have been out on the street awhile negotiating your own deals, setting your own budgets, and collecting your own revenues, you will begin to think with nostalgia of the simplicity and even beauty of your paycheck. You didn't even have to take it to your *bank*. Someone *else* made sure it was deposited on time. Someone *else* made sure all your taxes were taken out and your IRA was growing properly. Someone *else* looked after your insurance needs. Someone *else* invested your profit-sharing for you, and made sure that you never lost and almost always gained. Most important: You could always count on getting your paycheck with a known amount on a specific date. You could take it all for granted.

You now realize that those "bean counters" you hardly deigned to speak to did a lot for you. And you miss them. You can't help but miss them. For you went out to open an exciting, fulfilling new business—not to be a money manager. You had a vision of yourself conquering new worlds, not spending time trying to collect old receivables. Yet when you become an entrepreneur, just getting paid becomes a major challenge.

The truth strikes you within weeks: If you can't manage your money successfully, you can't stay in business.

When Your Customer Doesn't Pay

It will happen to you. It has happened to all of us. It is part of the learning process of any new entrepreneur.

An entrepreneur described his first experience this way: "I was so pleased to get my first client. He asked me to do an analysis of a particular product. I didn't just give him an analysis, I gave him a complete marketing plan. Including every possible permutation—as well as specific suggestions on how he might distribute the product. I went far and away beyond what he had asked for because it was my first job, and I wanted to make sure I exceeded his expectations. I thought that was the best way of assuring more business.

"I spent six weeks on it, working late nights and weekends. I delivered it on time, and went over the whole report with my client. He was extremely enthusiastic. He was, indeed, impressed by how much work I had done.

"Then I sent in my bill. We had agreed on a certain figure, and that was the one I used—although I had far exceeded my original estimate in the sense of how much time it actually took me.

"Six months later, I had still not received a dime. Finally I went in person to see my client. He was obviously embarrassed. He told me that his company had decided *not* to go ahead with the new product, and thus he could not put any costs against it. He said he had not cleared my involvement, or the involvement of any other outside consultant, with his boss. He was so sure the project would go forward, he had not bothered to ask anyone for permission to hire for this project.

"But he could get fired if he now asked them for some money. They wouldn't give him the money, and they would think he had made a mistake. No one wanted anything to do with that idea anymore. Even raising the idea could get him in trouble.

The bottom line was that the only way I was going to get any money from him was if he paid for it himself, and he couldn't afford to do that.

"As he talked with me, he became progressively more angry—as though it were my fault for not having been more professional. He told me I should not have done any work for him without a *signed estimate.* That was the professional way to go, he said. That would have forced him to clear it with his boss, and then we wouldn't have to be having this conversation. He said that he had made a mistake in hiring me, but I had made an even bigger one by not agreeing to the arrangement in a more professional manner.

"He ended the meeting by asking his secretary to show me out. It was the most humiliating professional experience of my life.

"I had *lost* a good client, and *not* been paid. An unbeatable combination. I have thought about it a lot, and I think it all started with my not putting together a more formal, professional financial document in the first place. If I had, I might still be working with him, and with his company."

His story is not unique.

Successful entrepreneurs always insist on some form of agreement, even if it is just a simple letter confirming a conversation. A letter can be a nonthreatening way to confirm a verbal contract.

Verbal agreements can always be fudged or misunderstood. When situations change—and they do almost daily in business—it is easy for people to edit their memories in a way that makes them look good and you look stupid. That's why it is a great help for any entrepreneur to understand the first law of having your own business: When you are going to be investing your time and/or money in any effort, make sure you have a clear agreement with your client—and confirm it in writing beforehand.

Ex Post Facto Is a No-No

Bringing up the issue of money after the fact, after the job has been done, is a no-no.

There are many corporations today that will not begin a job without an estimate. When you were an employee, you might have thought that this was more of the paper-pushing bureaucracy at work. Actually, in this case, it is wise to follow that lead. Begin no work without an explicit written understanding of what that work will involve and how much you will be paid and when you will be paid.

Yet many new entrepreneurs find it extremely difficult to ask anyone for money. An entrepreneur we talked to actually went to a therapist to see if she could get some help in being more financially assertive before she went out on her own. The therapist listened to her tale of being afraid to ask anyone for money. Then the therapist told her that this was a common feeling—among employees. But as soon as someone was out on her own and had to make money to survive, the need to ask for money overcame the early inhibitions.

"When your own survival is at stake," the therapist told her, "you will find that you are confident, almost eager, to ask for money." The therapist also told her that he was sure she would have no trouble. "You have been a successful corporate executive, fighting your way up in a tough, competitive environment. You are a strong person and will surprise yourself at your ability to be strong and upfront about your financial needs." And he was right. Once out of the corporate environment, she was naturally and effectively able to perform.

Being financially assertive is essential for survival. For even the biggest and best of Fortune 500 companies can keep you waiting. It has happened to many entrepreneurs.

A Good Beginning Doesn't Count

An entrepreneur we interviewed built a company whose specialty was supplying packaging, and he was pleased to get the business of several Fortune 500 companies. He did the packaging. They were pleased with his efforts and used his designs. He had expected that his business would be successful if he could get some good customers and do some excellent work for them.

He had accomplished those two early goals. But he forgot the punch line for any business transaction: Did you get paid?

An entrepreneur, unlike an employee, cannot afford to "donate" his time or energies or give away anything he makes. And every new entrepreneur quickly realizes that the success of every effort is determined, in the end, by whether or not you make money on that expenditure of energy.

It seems so obvious, yet it is still a surprise to most to encounter the irrefutable fact that the best beginning in the world cannot overcome a bad ending. Or even overcome a business relationship that includes an extended period of waiting.

Every day you wait to get paid puts you in the position of being a banker for your customer. It stretches your resources and endangers your ability to continue and to invest in new opportunities for your business.

The waiting game is a dangerous game to play.

There Ought to Be a Law

And he discovered the dangerous agony of this situation as he waited. For days. And then weeks. Nothing. After a month, he called to make sure they had received his invoice. He was assured that they had.

Another month went by. He was getting hungry. And it wasn't just the money, he told himself, but it was the need for reassurance that he had done the job well. Eventually, painfully, he realized that a good beginning simply doesn't count when it comes to getting paid. Finishing up by being paid is the only way to stay in business. He thought to himself: "There ought to be a *law* so that all bills have to be paid within thirty days." This is especially true when you have a small supplier or company dealing with a much bigger company. There is a built-in inequality to that situation that often encourages the larger company to withhold funds from a smaller company.

And this entrepreneur is probably right. There ought to be a law. But there is no law. So you need a good accountant to get the money for you.

Count on Someone Who Can Count

He turned for help to a good accountant. The accountant sympathized. He understood the need to eat. And he also gave our friend an interesting insight into corporate America.

"Don't take it personally," he said. "All these corporate financial snooks have been told to hold payment for ninety days. That's their whole life. If they can collect from their suppliers the money in thirty days, and don't have to pay out for ninety days, they can go to the CEO and claim they are a profit center. Big deal. Don't worry, I'll call them."

The accountant called his fellow accountants over at the big corporation. It was a help that they knew that he was also—like them—an accountant. And they leveled with him. The accountant discovered that our friend hadn't gotten stamped by the bureaucracy as an "approved supplier." You have to be an "approved supplier" before any check can be cut by many major corporations.

Even then, they like to hold the money up. They didn't send the check immediately, but it did arrive within the month. But the main thing his accountant gave him was an *insight* into how money is used. He cleared away some of the mystery, and helped him eat. He is still fulfilling that function . . . every day. The entrepreneur was lucky to find him.

For it is not only with big customers that you will need a good accountant. Even smaller customers can take months to pay—without the nudging of a proper financial perspective.

Just one of the key dimensions a good accountant can provide.

When a "No" Can Save Your Business

Jeffrey Sellon, an entrepreneur who built an amazingly successful business offering supplementary teaching materials to schools, told us, "I value my accountant most of all—he tells me when I can spend money. I get excited about a lot of projects, but you've got to figure out whether you can make money—before you start. Your accountant is the guy who tells you that you can afford it, or that you should wait six months. And if you don't listen you are in deep trouble.

"Most entrepreneurs tend to be optimists. Most accountants tend to be pessimists. When it comes to money, it's best to be pessimistic—then you make conservative forecasts. You don't hire a lot of people, or take on a lot of fixed costs, and then have to figure out why you are going broke."

And this is precisely what happened to two entrepreneurial partners in an international distribution business. Their business was growing; they kept investing. They had agreed to help distribute products for some major companies. But these companies, because of the size and scale of their operations, were used to dealing in major amounts of product. Thus, our optimistic entrepreneurs had to set up a major distribution network—which took a lot of money. Yet the payout could be immense, so they went ahead. And they went ahead—at least in part—because of an accountant who had given them inaccurate advice. The accountant looked over the books and concluded that they were making money, more than breaking even. What the accountant had not taken into account was that they were borrowing large sums that were geared to interest rates that might rise. The interest rates did rise. In addition, the partners were hit with taxes that the accountant had not anticipated. The rise in interest rates, combined with the rise in taxes, brought on a crisis situation.

Yet the whole situation didn't become clear until the end of a year. It was like a dream that ended as a nightmare. At year-end it was too late to do anything but scramble to others for financial assistance. The partners had to sell out at a loss. They had—with these accounting mistakes—snatched financial defeat from the jaws of victory. The lesson: A bad accountant can put you out of business.

Many entrepreneurs lose their business simply because they overestimate revenue, underestimate expenses. A good accountant can track the flow of money so that you don't make such fatal mistakes.

A Tiny Profit Can Build a Big Business

Frank Quirk, an entrepreneur we interviewed, told us about Macro International, a company he has helped build with a specific business philosophy. Macro does a lot of work with the federal government. To work with the federal government and manage to make money, you need the input of a great accountant and a great accounting system.

The pretax profit in this business averages six percent of sales. That's the bad news. The good news is that, if the company performs well, the government always pays and Macro almost always makes a profit.

As Macro has won more and more contracts, it has given Frank and his partners the opportunity to employ more people and invest in the business, confident of the payout.

Because of the excellence of the financial system, they were also able to grow by buying other entrepreneurial companies that were not as profitable or as secure. Many entrepreneurial companies simply cannot even match six percent pretax margin or look forward to a secure future. But under the new arrangement with Macro, they were happy to be acquired by a management that had a track record of knowing how to make money in the most challenging situations.

In sum, the partners at Macro have found a way of managing the finances so that they have been able to build a very successful business with great growth and security. The company has grown from three million dollars only twelve years ago to over fifty million of gross revenue today.

Frank says: "My short-term agenda comes from my monthly financial statement. It tells me where we are, what we need to do, and helps me find hundreds of ways for us to make a little money. And a little money made in a lot of little ways every day adds up to big money in the end."

On the other hand, a lot of little losses incurred every day can sink even the biggest of big ideas. That is one of the big surprises for many entrepreneurs. They expect their ideas to carry the day. But in business, it can be the financial underpinnings for those ideas that allow them to live and grow.

That financial care and concentration on the bottom line can best be provided by an accountant who becomes the greatest friend your business ever had. He can show you how to turn an idea into a *profitable* idea. And that is, at the end of the day, the difference between a successful and an unsuccessful business.

Your bottom line, especially your profit line, is your important score. A profitable bottom line not only allows you to stay in business, it allows you to invest in and build your business.

So how can you find a good accountant?

How to Hire a Trustworthy Accountant

There is really only one way to find an accountant, and that is to begin a methodical search. This is not a task you should approach casually. Your whole business might ride on finding the right person.

You might start by asking a friend who is happy with her accountant—especially if that friend is in a similar business. You don't want to have an accountant at the low end of a learning curve; any accountant you interview should already be familiar with your business.

You should also start your search at the top of any particular accounting firm. Whatever the size of your business, you want some involvement from the top people.

And you should always interview more than one possible accountant. The interview should include a chance to get to know your prospective accountant as a person.

Once you have a recommendation of a possible accountant, offer to take him to lunch. Lunch will tell you whether you'd like to spend a lot of time with him. During lunch, you can also test his knowledge of your business by bringing up two or three possible problems. It is important that you ask your questions in the right format, a framework of questions that reflects real business issues for you.

You will get a good sense of his professional expertise, as well as determining whether the chemistry is right.

Remember the math teacher you really liked, the one who made math understandable, even fun? That is the kind of accountant you are looking for.

Which leads to another quality your accountant should have: He should be hungry. Don't get someone who has already made it. The ideal is to look for a tiger, running his own entrepreneurial business and willing to help you build your business for his account. And then always be ready to hold him to the highest standards. It is a matter of your survival. You have to be tough about letting things slide.

You Have to Be Unforgiving

An entrepreneur told us: "My first accountant was a passive type. It wasn't that he was lazy so much as the fact that he didn't help me anticipate problems. And once he made a mistake. One mistake from an accountant is one too many. I fired him. Having an accountant that makes mistakes is like having a brain surgeon who makes a mistake. One mistake can kill a small business."

Once you've got an excellent accountant, get ready to learn.

"Anyone Can Make Money"

Protected by our steady paychecks in our big-company cocoon, we used to say to ourselves: "Anyone can make money." It is so easy to gain the impression that money is a simple subject to understand when you are plotting your financial life with bi-monthly paychecks.

One of the biggest surprises in moving from employee to entrepreneur is the whole new dimension of financial focus you will have to acquire. When you go out on your own, the financial variables multiply many times over. And the magic of a profit is often a frustrating and elusive goal. Late payments, promised jobs that don't come through, orders that don't arrive, employees who leave, others who demand instantaneous raises, investments that turn sour, and overheads that seem impervious to any negotiation—all these factors combine for a confusing array of potential hazards. For now you must not only manage your own finances, you must manage the finances of an entire organization.

You have to learn to estimate capital expenditures, cash flow, and receivables. Above all, you have to begin to understand what work done in what way can actually drop some precious profit to your bottom line.

Even in the simplest of companies—a two-person operation in a service business, such as consulting (one of the fastest-growing entrepreneurial areas)—the financial variables become incredibly complex very, very quickly.

One example: It is surprising how much money you really need to succeed.

How Much Money Do You Need?

Eric Stein, a partner and chief financial officer of Macro International, a company we cite as being particularly aware of the need for strong financial controls, gave us some sound advice. He taught us a simple approach to determining what he calls our capital requirement. We call it "our nut," as in how much money will it take to make this mighty oak grow.

His advice was focus first on how much outgo will go out

before income comes in, because insufficient capital is the most commonly given reason for business failures. Here is a step-by-step way where everybody, including the mathematically challenged, can calculate how much money it will take to create a profitable business.

1. Estimate your expenditures for the first year of your business on a monthly basis:

   a. Total your indirect costs. Indirect costs, or fixed costs, are those costs that stay the same no matter how much you sell except when you make significant expansion to your business. These costs are rent, utilities, health insurance, employee salary. Don't forget payroll taxes. Put these costs down for each of the twelve months of the first year of your business and total the costs.

   b. Calculate your direct costs. These are the costs related to the product or service you are selling. If you are selling a product, what is the cost of producing the product (e.g., purchasing the widgets and components prior to your selling them to a customer)?

   If your product is a service and you are the cost, then compute your direct costs per hour by taking your annual desired target salary and dividing by 2,080 (40 hours per week by 52 weeks), or if you plan to take a two-week vacation, dividing by 2,000 hours (40 hours per week by 50 weeks). This gives you the cost of an hour of your labor.

   Estimate how many hours of the 2,080 you will devote to working on the projects and multiply by the cost per hour to get your direct cost per month. For example, if you want to make $62,400 for your first year, then your hourly wage is $30.00 per hour ($62,000 ÷ 2,080).

If your annual projection assumes that you will be working with clients for 50 percent of your time and the other 50 percent marketing your service, the direct cost for your time is $31,200 for the first year.

    c. Total your indirect and your direct costs.

    d. Calculate these costs on a monthly basis.

2. Conservatively estimate your expected revenue by month and for your year based upon when the check will be received. Remember that most companies take between 60 and 90 days to pay.

3. Deduct the expected revenue from your costs by month. This is your nut—otherwise known as the working capital required to fund your business for one year.

You will be shocked when you calculate how much money you will need to get your business up and going. For example, a two-person service company with one part-time employee and modest indirect costs of $53,000 per year will need annual revenue of almost $180,000 per year ($15,000 per month) in order to pay each partner $62,400 (assuming 50 percent billability).

Additionally, when you calculate your working capital needs by month, you will be surprised to find that the cost of getting your business up and going will grow each month until it finally peaks when your cash flow catches up and you begin to make a profit. You must have the money put aside to cover this necessary start-up investment.

Don't Trust Former Colleagues Just Because You Knew Them in Corporate Life

A now wiser and more successful entrepreneur told us this story: "When I departed my corporation, I was able to take with me a nice chunk of cash. Naturally, I wanted to invest it and make it grow.

"Unfortunately, one of my self-employed former colleagues heard that I was in a position to invest in his business. He gave me a business plan that looked plausible. Because we were old friends, I didn't involve my accountant in the discussions. I should have. I had known my friend for more than twenty years and considered him completely honest. I should have known better.

"When it comes to money, even your best friends will deceive you. I really should have had an accountant to act as a buffer, and filter all money issues through his skeptical gaze. Your accountant can be a perfect excuse for you not to invest in your friends' financially uncertain ventures. Just because someone is a good friend does not mean they represent a good investment.

"I learned the lesson the hard way—by spending my hard-earned money for it. The business projections he gave me were *hopes* rather than *realities*. I am *still* waiting for any returns."

Don't Trust Yourself to Beat the IRS

We have heard of numerous instances in which companies in a cash flow bind use their payroll deduction to carry them over, and in the worst instance of this practice have been closed down by the Internal Revenue Service. It seems illogical that the IRS would close a business down, because that means the IRS would lose all hope of ever getting paid. But the IRS is a blunt instrument, a bureaucracy that focuses more on enforcing rules today than on what will happen tomorrow. If you owe the IRS money, it will approach collection as a dog approaches a bone.

In addition, if you "borrow" money from the funds you are supposed to put in the payroll deduction of your employees, the IRS regards this as stealing. It sees this money as not your money to give or to take, but rather the money of your employees.

One entrepreneur we talked to got in trouble just this way. He started a small business, ran into a cash flow problem, and used some of the money that was supposed to go to the payroll deductions of his employees. The IRS caught him. He made it good—almost immediately. But the IRS never let up. It hounded him out of business.

Don't trust yourself to beat the IRS. The IRS is an octopus you can't reason with and don't want to wrestle with over your finances.

The wisest rule with the IRS is to keep it as far away from your business as possible. For most entrepreneurs, this means playing the game the IRS's way, and using your innovative powers to move your business forward in other areas.

Don't Trust Yourself

Some bad money decisions come from simply trusting in your own optimistic projections. Most people who become self-employed are incurable optimists—otherwise they would never have left their comfortable corporate job. An entrepreneur we interviewed confidently set up an architectural firm. He had many promised projects and many more possibilities of commissions. He rented a large space and hired several assistants.

One of the projects did, indeed, come through. But another one was delayed. And a third took much longer than expected. All in all, he ended the year with a small loss. But the next year, to him, looked even brighter. He was getting more and more inquiries about his work. He now had some buildings to show prospects. He expected it to be an even better year. So he kept the big space and he didn't lay off any of his assistants. In fact, he took the opposite approach: He fired an accountant who told him that he was overoptimistic in his projections. In effect, he fired the messenger of bad news. He wanted an accountant who was a cheerleader rather than a realist.

After two years, he was substantially in debt. What would and could have been a flourishing business became, instead, an unprofitable one—simply because of the overoptimistic, unrealistic behavior of the leader. And his unwillingness to listen to his accountant.

Today, he has found an accountant to whom he is willing to pay attention—and together they are moving forward. He is more successful than he ever thought he'd be. And, as he says, "I could never have done it if I hadn't started to listen to a good accountant." And that his how it has to be.

Your optimism has got to be tempered with reality. Once again, that's where your faithful friend, your accountant, can come in. Your accountant can do a reality check on your projections. Since accountants usually take a more pessimistic view, the actual reality is often somewhere between your positive perception and his more negative calculation. But the *very act of talking to your accountant* can clear the air.

And it is always better to *take a cautious view of your cash flow*. Many entrepreneurs have gone down the tubes not because they didn't get business, but because their expenses always exceeded their revenues.

One Percent Is All It Takes to Fail

If your expenses exceed your revenues by just one percent, you are going to fail. That's a scary fact—especially to those of us from the corporate world who are used to traveling first class.

Today, most successful entrepreneurs we know fly steerage and stay at the cheapest hotels (as long as they are safe). Many have learned that every nickel spent means that at least ten need to be earned. That is literally the proportion in your financial life. That's equivalent to a ten percent profit margin, which is doing very well as an entrepreneur. When you consider your overhead, your limited time, and your future obligations, that is the reality you must always have before you.

Many entrepreneurs expect to write off all their expenses. And that sounds like a wonderfully expansive way to live. But that lifestyle is only possible if your expenses are *less* than your revenues. If your expenses are even one percent higher than your revenues, you are on your way out of business. It's only a matter of time.

That is why you must set up a system that gives you a good look at your profit and loss—every business day. You might think this is not necessary, but it is. Knowing where you are every day can be the difference between building a successful business and going out of business.

The more you have to guess at your bottom line, the more financial danger you are in. At any moment, your great idea that you are working so hard to make a reality could be mortally wounded by an imbalance between the money you earn and the money you spend. Every day that you're one percent ahead is a day you're doing great; if you're one percent behind, you're in deep weeds.

It is your primary job, as an entrepreneur, to make sure you have a clear, daily picture of your profits. Of course, this clear financial sight takes effort—and time.

You Have to Invest Your Time to Make Sure You Make Money

Time might be money, but an even more important point to consider is this: Money takes time. You have to spend time learning about it and counting it, and you have to spend time in negotiating your deals. Your time is extremely valuable. You have to learn to think of your time as an *essential investment.* Make sure you *make money* out of all your efforts. Almost every client arrangement for a self-employed person will be unique. In our years outside, we haven't done a single deal that's *exactly* like another one. So it takes time to understand, working with your accountant, how you can structure a deal so that you make something out of all the time you will be expending. And then you have got to expect also that a certain percentage of your deals will go bad. Enter your need for a good lawyer.

Taking Advantage of a Good Lawyer

"Lawyers are the mystery of my life. I've dealt with many law firms—some are better, some are worse, but all are expensive."

—Tom Margittai

Finding a good lawyer is just as important as finding a good accountant. You can ask friends, but it is not as simple as that. You have got to take command of the situation *or you can go broke getting the help you need.* Lawyers are really expert at making you pay enormous sums for their advice. Even reputable lawyers can charge you outlandish amounts of money—in just a few hours of talk.

And while lawyers love to talk, they hate to talk about money. They would prefer it if you never raised the issue and they could just send you a huge bill at the end of the experience.

Yet an open-ended discussion with a lawyer can be a financial disaster for you. So you have to be very, very careful with lawyers. We have a three-step process we have worked out that helps us *take advantage of lawyers—before they take advantage of us:*

1. We ask for a written proposal of how they would handle the *particular* case we bring them. We don't want generalities here—we want ideas.
2. We ask for a *specific* estimate of how much it will cost us to go forward to a successful *conclusion* of our case. We want to put our lawyer in a box so that it is in his or her interest to re-solve—rather than prolong—the case.

   Note: Some lawyers will charge a fee to prepare an esti-mate. The lawyers' rationale for this first fee is for the time they spend in understanding your case enough to prepare an accurate estimate. So before you even talk with a lawyer, make sure you prepare your notes as carefully as possible. And limit your conversation to between ten and fifteen minutes. (Many lawyers charge by five-minute increments.)

3. We always ask *three* lawyers. We have found that there is usually a pattern to their advice, and yet often a wide range in fees. So we can move confidently forward in a particular direction based on the advice, and take the lawyer with the lowest proposed fee. Again, you might have to pay a minimum fee just to receive this first advice, but we feel it is worth it. A relatively small investment at the beginning of your relationship with a lawyer can save you many thousands later.

Getting a proposal, with a budget, from three lawyers, can be very enlightening. You become your own best advocate under those conditions. And that is what you *have* to be. For lawyers, unlike most accountants, love to stir up trouble. However, *the problems they create cost fortunes to resolve.* That's why lawyers can become the *enemies* of the struggling entrepreneur. In the next life, we should all either go to law school or abolish all lawyers. Right now, it is important to discover how to use them to your advantage.

So make sure *you* are in charge of your case. Decide on a process and a fee—in advance. Even then, only call the lawyers in when you and your accountant have failed. They will almost always cost you as much as you gain.

One way to stay abreast of the legal fees is to ask for monthly billings. And realize that no matter what the subject you are discussing with your lawyer, the meter keeps ticking. You must remember it's the lawyer's livelihood. Some people think they are having a friendly conversation on the phone, and then they get billed for it. Expect such behavior from your legal counsel and you won't be surprised or disappointed. You'll learn to watch your watch. Yet you will still be surprised at how long some things can take.

And that is why estimating the cost of any action involving lawyers can be tricky. Time goes by, and the costs mount.

An entrepreneur we talked to had a small company that agreed, for a small percentage, to help set up a big conference. The conference was a smashing success. To help achieve that success, his small company had run up out-of-pocket costs and time totaling over forty-six thousand dollars. The conference sponsors claimed that there was never even a verbal agreement, and refused to pay. This was an untruth—there had been a clear verbal agreement that he would be reimbursed for all his costs. They even shook hands on it. Yet now they told him he should be grateful just to have been a part of such a major undertaking, and expected him to make his money back by all the valuable "contacts" he would make at the conference.

He talked to a lawyer. The lawyer advised him to take them to court. He pressed the lawyer for an estimate. The lawyer resisted, emphasizing that once such an action began, it was difficult to estimate the amount of time required to successfully prosecute it.

Finally, the lawyer told him that such an action might cost as much as fifty thousand dollars. In addition, the lawyer charged him an immediate five-thousand-dollar fee for his counseling so far and asked for a retainer of ten thousand dollars more.

Our entrepreneur decided not to proceed. His thinking: "*You might be morally right, but it is better to be pragmatic.* Why spend more money than you can make for the pleasure of being proved right?"

He approached the conference sponsors with a proposition: He would settle his claim without a suit for twenty-six thousand dollars. That was the money he had had to lay out to pay his outside suppliers. He was willing to give up billing anything for his own time.

They settled with him.

He still feels that it was better to settle and be assured of some cash than unleash a legal battle he was not sure of winning.

Entrepreneurs learn to avoid legal actions that can take their time as well as their money. Money is too hard to get to let it go in legal fees.

Just ask your banker.

How to Beat Your Banker at His Own Game

"A banker: the person who lends you his umbrella when the sun is shining and wants it back the minute it rains."

—*Mark Twain*

A headhunter for the health-care business had a successful operation that took in more than a million dollars a year. She went to her bank for the simplest of loans: a loan to extend her available credit. They turned her down when they heard she was self-employed.

Although she was angry with their reaction, she didn't do anything.

But then an employee of hers went to the same bank. He asked for an extension of the credit on his existing account, and he got it. He had no problem because he could put down on the application that he was an employee, and that he had had his job for more than two years.

The successful entrepreneur became furious. An employee of hers could get a loan, but she could not.

She went to the bank. They explained to her that, yes, they regarded self-employed people as higher credit risks than employees. They also said they were particularly suspicious of self-employed people who had been in business for less than five years. She insisted on seeing the manager of the bank. She was finally able to get her loan, but not until she had a major fight and supplied an incredible amount of documentation. She was clearly fighting against the grain, going against a whole carload of policies that had been built up over many years and followed in a mindless fashion.

And banks are famous for carrying out policies that no longer make sense.

Yet it is wise, even essential, that you understand where your local banker is coming from. Bureaucratic rules and written policies loom large in bankers' lives.

Denis Gouey was beginning a business in a unique yet growing field: He was to open a one-person operation to save and restore priceless manuscripts to their former glory.

What could be more needed by great collectors? He already knew there was a market for his services, and he had already established relationships with some of the most noted collectors and bibliophiles in the world. These tended to be people of great wealth.

Yet, in thinking about his needs, he decided that it would be wise to take out a ten-thousand-dollar loan. He knew that he would need some money to set up a shop, and he wanted some as a cushion for possible late-paying clients. (Being very rich people, his clients sometimes forget the importance of prompt payment of such "small" bills.)

He decided to go to his local bank, where he had banked for eleven years. He was greeted cordially. He explained his plans for his new business. He showed the loan officer a list of clients who had already commissioned his work—including a sprinkling of people who are numbered among the Forbes 400 richest people in the world. He said that his needs were minimal, but that he thought he should have a financial cushion to take care of any unexpected expenses. The loan officer was enthusiastic about his plans. But he said that the bank never gave out less than two hundred and fifty thousand dollars for entrepreneurial operations.

"It's just not worth our time to do the paperwork on anything less," the loan officer said.

Denis said, "I had to work twice as hard in starting my business to earn enough to pay for setting up shop and supporting my professional needs. But I did it—without the help of my banker."

Today, Denis is the one of the most respected and successful people in his field. Yet his early struggle with his bank makes a key point: Bankers literally live by *policies* and paperwork. Their careers are determined by how well they follow the policies set down by the higher-ups. While you might be able to find an individual banker who is willing to break the rules, it is easier to go with the banker's corporate culture.

So it is important to understand those policies, and beat the the bankers at their own game. And here is how to do that: Because bankers are eager to lend you money before you need it when you still have plenty of assets, that is the *ideal* time to get it. Why get money when you are least in need of it? Because, as sure as you are an entrepreneur, you will need it later.

It is the experience of even the most successful entrepreneurs that they needed at least two years, or the equivalent, of overhead—which includes, for example, your salary, any rent to be paid, and any expenses for equipment.

As you read this you might be thinking: "But this is nonsense. I am sure I will make money within two years."

Trust us. And the hundreds of entrepreneurs whose stories we've heard. No matter how well you do or what business you are in, you will need to budget for at least two years of expected overhead. There are *no* exceptions to this rule.

Cash flow will inevitably be a problem, and having two years of money in the bank can allow you to build your business in a professional way without having to panic or go under just as you are beginning to succeed.

This money in the bank will also give you a psychological edge in any negotiations. You will be able to fight harder for what you really want to do, rather than take on jobs simply to keep yourself going (a major danger we will discuss in an upcoming chapter).

The easiest and best time to get this money from your banker is when you are still perceived as a creditworthy employee. *Go to your banker while you are still employed.* Bankers will be reassured by your paycheck stubs, your home, and your car. They will be eager to lend to you.

Borrow as much as you can, over the longest period of time with the lowest possible fixed interest rate (you can't afford the upward swing of interest rates as you are getting started). The bigger your loan, the more the odds increase that you will be able to make it through those crucial early years. And the more you borrow, the more the bank will have a stake in your success.

Once you become an entrepreneur, it will be much harder to raise this kind of cash. So do it while you fit the bankers' profile of a good credit risk.

Bankers can also be a source of good, free business information. Once you are a major borrower, they will be happy to help you analyze business trends and send you documents it would take you weeks to prepare.

They will also give you tips about how to handle your money. For once you have your pile of cash, you must treat it with respect. Money might not be the reason you went into business—but it is the primary reason you might fail.

Financial Success Means Taking Control

With all this talk of expert help—accountants and lawyers and bankers—we don't want to imply that *you* will be exempt from becoming an expert on how to deal with money. Successful entrepreneurs learn how to manage the relationships with bankers, lawyers, and accountants—but they also learn to take the whole subject of money as their *personal* responsibility. This is a subject you can't delegate and you can't afford to fail.

Money is the key to your success. Money is the lifeblood of *your* business. You will have to take it *personally.* You will have to make some tough calls to some nasty people to get paid. You will have to learn to negotiate in a way that makes sure that you come out a little bit ahead of your client. You will have to become the cheapest person you know.

You will have to begin to think in terms of dollars and cents in a way you never had before. You will begin to dream about money the way you dreamed about overdue term papers when you were in college. Remember those vague, unresolved anxieties? And then you woke up and realized it wasn't a dream. You were actually living with a lot of vague, unresolved anxieties. Money will be a thread of ominous anxiety in your every moment. But you will also begin to feel a new sense of power and self-esteem as you realize that you are truly in control of your financial destiny. Nothing is more exhilarating than the realization that you can make money by doing work that you love.

Successfully managing your business relationships, while making money doing what you enjoy, is one of the great pleasures of life.

Jeffrey Sellon sums it up best: "Making a living as an entrepreneur is dramatically different than earning a living as an employee. And a hell of a lot more fun! But you have to have some help—especially in the financial area. Accountants, to me, are the most important. Lawyers are a necessary evil that I try to use as little as possible due to their cost. Bankers are your problem. They are unwilling to take the risks that are necessary to your business. You have to be your own banker as much as possible—funding your growth out of your resources and the profits you generate. Don't take your eye off the bottom line—that's the way to build your business. Making money is only the beginning. If you can't learn to manage your money and find the right people to manage it for you, you can't survive."

One of the biggest surprises of entrepreneurial life is that early success, unless there is a profit that drops immediately to your bottom line, can put you out of business faster than any other single factor. Which is the subject of our next chapter.

How Success Can Derail Your Dream

"Too much success too early can cause you to grow overconfident, overextend yourself, and blow away your business."

> —*Mickey Garrett, whose business, Mickey Garrett Associates, grew so fast he almost lost control*

When you are sitting in a large corporation and beginning to plan your escape to the life of the entrepreneur, you build up an almost irresistible picture of what your new life will be like. You see yourself freed from office politics, administrative hassles, able to build a successful business by concentrating with a liberating energy on what you truly love to do.

It is easy for you to spend all your time thinking about how to assure your success, and hard, if not impossible, for you to consider why success of any kind would be dangerous. Your only hope is that you *will* succeed; you hardly pause to consider how to plan for success before it happens.

Yet it will be true for you, as it is for virtually all entrepreneurs, that success itself is not so easy to plan for. It can often be an entrepreneur's biggest challenge.

For the reality of success is very different from anything you might have had in mind.

The Surprises of Success

Surprise #1: Too Much Success Too Soon Can Sink Your Business

The *Wall Street Journal* recently headlined a story: PICTURE THIS! A FIRM FAILING FROM TOO MUCH SUCCESS. The story began: "When Harvey Harris started selling elaborate cut-rate personalized calendars in 1992, he anticipated strong demand. But not so strong that it would ruin him."

Harris explained what happened to him: "I'm a salesman, and a good one, that started this company up, and it exploded."

A good new product can often become a hot property that can overwhelm the ability of the entrepreneur. Harris's product was based on a technology that allowed people to virtually design their own calendars, with their favorite photographs.

When demand took off, the equipment upon which the new technology depended began to fail from overuse. He tried to buy additional equipment—but it was not enough. Quality suffered. And orders piled up. Tens of thousands of orders went unfilled.

He was also unable to collect revenues fast enough to pay for the new machines and set up the new systems that were needed. He fell more and more behind.

Until he had to close his business.

The business failed because it was not able to handle such great success. Harris might have been able to fill a "reasonable" demand, but when his product took off, he was simply not prepared for it.

Lesson: Overwhelming success is not good news—especially when you are just starting out. For success requires, as it did in the case of Mr. Harris, greater and greater capital outlays.

Surprise #2: The Greater Your Success, the More Money You Need to Invest

One of the big surprises for many entrepreneurs is that the more successful they are, the more they have to *invest* in their business. And the terrible truth is that usually the costs of overhead—such as salaries and rents and the need to invest in new facilities—seem to occur *before* an increase in revenues.

One entrepreneur bought a resort in Vermont. He invested a lot in upgrading the resort. It became more successful. Which meant that he had to hire more people and invest even more in new facilities. The more successful he was, the more he seemed to spend his time going to the bank to ask for more money. At the end of the third year of great success he was deeper in debt than when he began.

Lesson: Don't expect growth to cure your financial problems. It will often simply compound them. Be prepared financially, so that the need for extra capital outlays does not come as a complete surprise.

Surprise #3: Your Success Can Separate You from What You Love to Do

Often one of the key reasons people go out on their own is so that they can spend their time doing what they really love to do, without worrying about those administrative and internal problems of most big corporations.

Yet a primary paradox of growth and success in the business you began is that such growth can often take you away from doing what you love. The more successful your business becomes, the more you become a delegator or even a director. You lose the pleasure of being a *doer,* as you become a *manager* of a growing organization.

Marilyn Burns, as mentioned earlier, is a successful entrepreneur who built a business on her love for teaching and her ability to help teachers teach better. She had a great time in the early years. She loved visiting schools, talking with teachers, and helping the kids learn.

But her business became more and more successful. More and more schools were asking for her help. She had to contract other people to go to the schools and help train the teachers.

Soon she was staying back at headquarters, managing the office support staff.

Her business became incredibly successful—by any measure except one. She was not doing what she loved.

She spent more time managing personnel, discussing financial issues with her accountant, or huddling with lawyers than she did with teachers or students. Her very success had taken her away from the activity she loved.

She decided that this was "simply unacceptable. Why start a business and then not be able to run it the way you want—so that you can do what you love?"

Today, she has invested in hiring professional managers who can run the growing operation, so that she can go back to doing what she loves. She realized—just in time—that her very success was keeping her from really living out her dream. And her story is not unique.

Surprise #4: You Won't Know Whether or Not You Are Successful Very Soon

It is tempting, when you are imagining your entrepreneurial life, to think of it in stark, dramatic terms: You will either succeed spectacularly or fail miserably. Going out on your own seems like such a big risk to you that it seems logical you would know immediately whether or not your great gamble paid off. You plan to be able to tell in a month or two.

Unfortunately, such a clear result is not possible for most entrepreneurs.

One entrepreneur had an experience that is typical. He started a business selling a proprietary research product to Fortune 500 companies. He went into this venture with three other partners. All four agreed that at the end of one year they would decide whether to go forward with their business or call it quits and return to corporate life.

One year seemed a generous allocation of time to determine their success or failure. In fact, they agreed among themselves that they might very well have a clear picture in just a few months.

Yet that is not the way things turned out. Entrepreneurial life, just as normal life, is not that simple. At the end of the first year they had done very well in attracting some top clients. They had received some excellent, lucrative contracts. Yet cash flow was a continuing problem, and because they were loath to charge too much during their first year, they decided only to pay themselves a minuscule salary.

In sum, in analyzing their first year, they were left with both good news *and* bad news. The good news was that they had attracted the kind of business they had hoped for. The bad news was they had not attracted quite enough of it to give them the kind of salaries they were expecting.

In grading the performance of their business, they could not give themselves anything as dramatic as an A or an F. Their performance was probably more equivalent to a B− or a C+. They were not failing dramatically, and they were not succeeding dramatically. They were doing very well in some areas and not so well in others.

After much discussion, they decided to give their venture another six months. At the end of that six months, things were equally unclear: They were still building a group of valuable clients, but they were still not progressing at the rate they had hoped.

They gave it another six months. Then another. And another. At the end of three years . . . the picture was still confused. Two partners dropped out, two others stayed. Today, two years later, they are looking forward to greater success tomorrow, yet they are still close to failing. In other words, they are still encountering an unclear reality, rather than a clear-cut, irrefutable outlook one way or the other.

Lesson: It isn't that easy to know if you are succeeding or failing. The odds are you will be part of a situation in which it is unclear, even after months or years, whether you are going to really make it big or not. Setting specific financial goals *before* you begin your new business is a way to avoid this unfortunate situation.

The Mission Statement: First Step in Planning to Make Your Dream Come True

At this point you might be saying to yourself: "This concern about success won't apply to me—I'm just going to have a little bed-and-breakfast, or simply a small consulting business." Yet it inevitably will apply to you. What we have found is that you've got to have a *plan*—a plan that is a thoughtful, pragmatic reflection of your own personal and professional definitions of success. As one entrepreneur told us, "Any plan, no matter how bad, is better than no plan."

Regardless of the kind or size of business, this is an essential truth that touches every entrepreneur. Without such a plan, you can succeed in many ways and yet fail faster than you ever believed.

Although many find it hard to imagine, too much success too early—without a plan—can sink a business quicker than any other single fundamental mistake. Such unplanned success can lead to business bankruptcy and, even worse, emotional bankruptcy as well.

Thus, although new entrepreneurs tend to fear failure rather than plan for success, it is wise to mentally prepare for what can happen so that you can create your own definition of success. (Isn't that why you wanted to be an entrepreneur in the first place?) In other words, you've got to decide *before* you begin your entrepreneurial venture where you want to end up—exactly what balance of personal and professional activities and rewards will spell success for *you.*

Successful entrepreneurs *choose a business they love and one that can grow in a way they enjoy.* They are able to do this because they start out with a clear vision of where they want to go. This process is known as *creating your mission statement.*

Defining your mission statement is the most critical *first* step in planning for your success. It summarizes what you want to achieve. (In the next chapter we deal with *how* you will achieve it, which we call a road map.)

Your mission statement is your business goal simply stated *in two sentences or less.* Your mission statement should describe the business you are in and what you hope to achieve. In addition, the best mission statements reflect a bold and positive attitude and ambition. They act as a catalyst for a company and help it to focus on a higher level of performance.

Here are some good examples of successful organizations that have been able to write their business mission statements in forceful yet focused sentences that clearly convey their objectives. In our review of their company literature and in talking with people from these companies, we believe their mission statements could be summarized in the following manner.

Hewlett-Packard says: "Our basic business purpose is to create information products that accelerate the advancement of knowledge and improve the effectiveness of people and organizations."

The J. Walter Thompson advertising agency created a mission statement of less than ten words: "To create the most effective, distinctive advertising for our clients."

Merrill Lynch & Company, Inc., has a mission statement that conveys its worldwide efforts: "Our mission is to be a client-focused, worldwide financial services organization, striving for excellence by serving the needs of individuals, corporations, governments and institutions. Our objective is to be the acknowledged leader in the value we offer our clients, the returns we offer our shareholders and the rewards we offer our employees."

Coca-Cola has expressed its goals this way: "As the world's largest beverage company, we refresh the world."

Disneyland has gotten its mission statement down to just three words: "We create happiness."

When it comes to creating your own mission statement, it is wise to think in terms of the shorter, the clearer; the bolder, the better.

Your mission statement becomes the *desired destination for all your efforts.* Your mission statement will help you to control and leverage your success. Your clearly defined mission statement will help you to *focus* on what you really want out of your entrepreneurial life.

Since you are an entrepreneur, your business *is* your life, so when you write your business mission statement, you must also consider your personal priorities.

To help give you some idea of the kind of mission statement you might choose, we will discuss some dramatic examples of different entrepreneurial missions. (Note: The majority of successful entrepreneurs have a clear mission statement. So the question is not whether you should have a mission statement; it is, rather, *which one* you should choose.)

Before you write your mission statement you will want to consider several personal as well as professional options.

Considerations Behind Successful Missions

Decide Whether You Want to Be Big or Small— Just Don't Get Caught in the Middle!

Remember: When you're a success, growth *happens,* so you've *got to choose how and where you want to grow.* No choice is making a choice itself—to grow in an undisciplined way.

The size your business will be is a decision that should be made up front because, as an entrepreneur, you will be faced with making decisions that will affect your growth on an hourly basis. They are choices that cannot be put off once you begin. For, as we have already seen, growth doesn't wait to be invited in, it often arrives before you're ready for it. It is important for you to *plan* what size and stature you want to achieve.

Before you do anything, you've got to decide if your business mission is to be either big or small. The humorist Robert Benchley once said: "The world is divided into two groups of people. Those who divide the world into two groups of people, and those who don't." For the sake of making a point, we think it is helpful, in this case, to divide the world into two groups of entrepreneurs: the big and the small.

In interviewing successful entrepreneurs we have become convinced: *There is no middle ground.* As you are developing your mission statement, be advised that your ambition should be either to build a major, high-volume business or, on the contrary, to be a high-margin niche operation where it's you, and you primarily, who really *is* the business, with limited overhead and few, if any, employees.

Paul Allen and Bill Gates, founders of Microsoft, decided early on that they wanted to build the biggest company in the software business. Allen and Gates had a clear vision at the very beginning that they wanted to create the most popular, helpful, and widely used software in the world. As far back as their original office in Albuquerque, New Mexico, Microsoft's mission statement seemed to be: "We set the standard." They wanted to set the standard for software, and they made sure their software was in every computer possible. Success and large size didn't just happen to Paul Allen and Bill Gates. They planned for it.

Martin Braid, another entrepreneur in the software business, has a very different-sized mission statement. "I simply want to create a great software product. I have no dreams of building a big software empire," he says. Martin is now creating a new software product that will help large companies manage their files in a more effective way. Martin is basically a one-person operation.

Another entrepreneur we talked to has an operation that is different from Martin's, but he is still very much in charge of every important aspect—and wants to keep it just that way. Christopher Little has built a major photography business, but he has no intention of becoming any bigger. He still takes all the pictures himself. He has limited overhead and limited headaches by keeping his company the size in which he can control every vital detail.

Christopher wants to be intimately involved in every photograph. And each shot he takes is an exciting work of art precisely because of his intense personal involvement. Christopher's mission statement could be defined as: "Living a life that will let me create the best photographs in the world."

The big operation Paul Allen and Bill Gates created and the small operations Martin Braid and Christopher Little created are all successful. These entrepreneurs made a clear decision, reflected in their mission statements, about whether they want to be big or small. And these entrepreneurs succeeded at achieving their very different missions.

Getting caught between big and small can be fatal. We have talked to many struggling entrepreneurs whose business is caught in the middle—too small to get the benefits and build the necessary infrastructure and cash flow they need, yet too big to avoid office politics and continual money problems. As one of them told us: "My biggest emotional crisis now is the size of my business. I'm a success in my field. I work with important clients. But the huge pressure on me to sustain a large firm, make a payroll that has grown to over thirty people, and still pay the government all the taxes it wants has me looking in the mirror in the mornings and asking: Is this what it's all about?

"I wonder whether I should have a firm of, say, eight—where I could know everybody well and be in charge and more completely in control. And probably make more money. I yearn for the days before I grew so big. A lot of the fun can go out of the business when you end up a victim of your own growth. Remember that old joke: In every fat person there is a thin one trying to get out. I feel that way about my own business now."

On the other hand, another successful entrepreneur, Mickey Garrett, has worked hard to keep his marketing business small and has a very different story: "I never wanted to become a *pris-*

oner of my overhead. Once I had built up to having eight people on staff. I had never planned to get that big. Suddenly I was spending more time managing my payroll than I was helping my clients. And with all that added personnel work, I had also added a lot of overhead. I had to pay for more computers, more office space, more insurance, and had to fill out a lot more government forms. I was becoming a prisoner of my overhead. I wasn't making any more money at the end of the day. In fact, I was making more when I was *smaller.*

"I realized that the bigger I was growing, the more money I was losing. I almost lost it—I almost lost control of the business I had worked so hard to build. I stopped this unprofitable growth just in time. I did it dramatically.

"I let six of the eight people go. Today, I run my business in the way I planned: It's big enough to give me a good lifestyle and let me spend time with my family, yet small enough not to make me the prisoner of my overhead.

"And I have more money than I ever expected. Yet I could have lost it all if I had gotten carried away with my own success."

The size of your business is one of the most important choices you will make, for it will determine the kind of projects you will want to take on and the kind of life you will live. And what you do with your time. If you become a large, high-volume player, you will spend a lot of time managing your staff, hiring and firing, and finding ways to motivate people to do more. If you are content to stay small, your major management challenge will be your own time and making sure that every assignment is one in which your particular skills will be displayed to the greatest advantage.

Being the biggest in your field or simply small and excellent is a key decision for you to make—a decision that involves a lot of planning. Either plan can work. But neither course should be embarked upon without a realistic assessment of the risks and rewards involved. And, of course, your decision should, above all, reflect your *feelings* about what you would like to do.

One of our entrepreneurial stories deals with a surprising fact: Many successful entrepreneurs do not plan to be the biggest—they simply plan to be the best at doing what they love. A successful entrepreneur decided she didn't have to be the biggest to be happy. She had a different definition of success . . .

Determine If You Can Be the Best at What You Love to Do

Ludmilla Ivanovic told us, "I never set out to be the biggest. I don't even like to think about competing in that way. And I don't want to be too big, anyway. My husband, Iggy, and I simply wanted to create the best bread we could for people, and create the bread in a happy environment. You could say that was our original mission statement."

We asked her if it hadn't taken great courage to set up a whole new business with her husband while she was expecting her first child.

"Courage?" she said, "My mother really had courage. She escaped from a German concentration camp when she was fourteen. When the Allied bombers came in and the Germans ran for the air raid shelter, she ran for the woods. She survived for weeks until the Americans rescued her. She had courage.

"Setting out to set up your own business in America today doesn't take the same kind of courage—lots of people are cheering you on. I would say I had more determination than courage. Once I became pregnant, I realized that we really had to build a business for ourselves. My husband and I weren't good at being employees. And we were barely making enough to live on. If we were going to have success, it would have to be doing something more creative—on our own."

She and her husband both had "day jobs" at E.A.T.—a top New York bakery and restaurant. She was an actress, and her husband was going to college—on the side. During the day they held down jobs as, respectively, a waitress and delivery driver. Now that they had decided they should build a business, they didn't have far to look for a good model. Together, they had watched E.A.T. grow on the strength of the great bread.

They decided they would like to open a bakery like E.A.T.— serving the finest bread possible. Yet they knew that New York was a very competitive city. And E.A.T. was already doing an excellent job of answering New York's need for delicious bread.

"I don't believe in competition," our friend says. "I believe in need."

So they went looking for a market that had a real *need* for great, freshly baked bread.

They visited the restaurants in Boston. Most of the restaurants were serving bland, prefrozen bread. The owners of the restaurants told them that they would be happy to carry their bread—if it was good enough.

On the strength of that market research, they moved to Boston. After much looking and many negotiations, they found a solid structure on a little street called Calvin, just on the edge of the city. They opened a bakery and called it Iggy's.

"It turned out that my husband had a genius at knowing how to create just the right-tasting bread," she says. "He was a scholar at college and now has become a scholar of what it takes to make exceptional-tasting bread. Believe it or not, making great bread takes a lot of thought and subtlety. Putting the right spices and ingredients together is like putting the right chords together to create a piece of music."

Her husband also, fortunately, discovered that he had an ability to understand and work with machinery—for baking takes a major investment in ovens and stirrers, and the modulation of the temperature is one of the key elements in producing just the right crust and texture for the bread.

While her husband concentrated on setting up the right ovens, Ludmilla called on hundreds of restaurants. "Our first winter, 1993, was record-breaking for the number of storms. It was a terrible winter," she says, "but each day I made my way through the snow and ice to talk to people. I was pregnant again, with one child in my arms. Maybe they took pity on me, but they were all very nice. At least they realized that I was the kind of person who would make it out—in any weather."

Ludmilla also brought them the first samples of her bread—which were enthusiastically received. "We only use natural organic flour and ingredients. We cook it fresh—each day," she says. "Those factors make it better than most breads. My husband, Iggy, supplies the artistic touch, I supply the love and positive energy, and we both have passionate natures. My friend India has gone to business school and helps manage everything—she has saved my business life many times. I try to make sure everyone is working in a positive, cheerful atmosphere with one goal: to make wonderful bread for people. We don't look on ourselves as trying to make a lot of money so much as to perform a service for others."

Iggy's became more and more popular. It was recently featured in *Boston* magazine as being the best bakery in that area. It is widely recognized as having the most passionate and inspired people creating great-tasting bread.

"Now we are confronting the temptation to expand," she says, "but my husband and I don't want to grow just to be big. We have many people working for us. We want to invest in them. We offer trips to visit bakeries in Paris. Maybe we will buy a new oven. We only want to make our bread in one location—we don't want to franchise our idea. We want to be involved in creating the dough, in tasting the bread—every day. We want to know our customers and be able to discuss each kind of bread with them.

"I want to make sure that we are giving people the best bread we can. We couldn't do that if we got involved in running some kind of worldwide business empire or trying to sell franchises. Making the best bread takes a personal, intimate involvement. It is like making love—you can't be thinking or doing something else at the same time."

Ludmilla and Iggy are successful because they started with a clear mission, a clear idea that they wanted to be the best at what they loved to do. They planned it just that way.

Understanding and planning for your own needs—as well as the needs of your business—is the surest way to succeed.

Decide What Kind of Lifestyle You Want

One entrepreneur had a very specific goal and a very clear definition of success: "I wanted the satisfaction of having my own business, being my own boss, but I also wanted to create a balanced lifestyle. My mission statement was to create a business that ensures a good lifestyle for me and my family.

"So I made sure I *planned* for this balanced lifestyle when I went into my entrepreneurial venture. I wanted to spend time with my family and take vacations when I wanted to. I was looking for a business that would allow me to be successful—without killing myself."

He had spent fifteen years working for an English bank, one of the biggest banks in the world. As he rose up the ladder, he had become more and more disenchanted with being an employee in a large organization.

"I found myself in so many meetings where people were actually yelling at each other. For some reason it got worse the further up you went. People seemed to become ever more critical . . . even vicious. Everyone spent so much time looking over each other's shoulders, it was a waste of time to me."

The big bank wanted him to move up in the corporate hierarchy and move to Germany. "Germany, like much of the world," our friend says, "is still very traditional at the higher reaches of business. You are put in a slot and expected to toe the line. It is a form of a class system that I didn't really enjoy—even when you're at the top. It takes the humanity out of life. Eventually I would have gotten a car and driver and everyone would have been very respectful. But I like to drive myself, and I don't need people bowing to me to make my day.

"Moving to Germany was also not something my family or I wanted to do on a personal basis. So we decided to plan for a better life for ourselves, by going into business for ourselves."

He was able to negotiate a good severance from the large English bank, and he also sold his house to raise more money—for he had decided to buy a successful small business.

"I wanted to find a business that was already doing well," he says. "I thought that would cut down on the risk. Also, I could bring a financial perspective that might help the business to grow."

He found a business broker to help him in his search. The broker recommended that he find a service business because of his career in banking.

They looked at food companies, including one making sausage. They also looked at other kinds of companies. The broker found a company outside Philadelphia that was doing very well in printing and publishing materials. This was a company that, although small, was providing a service to major companies such as AT&T, which were now outsourcing this kind of service.

"I was attracted by the fact that they had a solid business," he says. "But the most important single factor was the man who had built the business was an honest man. I knew from my days at the bank that no matter how carefully you investigate any investment, it all comes down to trusting somebody. I felt I could trust this man."

An honest seller is key to buying a business. And in this case the seller also had an excellent motivation. He had had a heart attack and he and his wife wanted to move to Tucson and enjoy life more. So he was eager to sell and was happy to find a buyer who would continue to treat his customers well.

Today, this entrepreneur has built the business he bought. He has kept the original clients and added more. He has invested in the high-tech equipment necessary to properly perform and still be a leader in speed and cost. His banking background gave him an excellent understanding of finances, so he has been able to plan growth in a profitable way.

"We don't want to become so big that I have to spend all my time at the office," he says. "I have about a dozen employees. One person is a wizard at the technology. Another is my manager—he makes sure the job gets done. I just put everyone on a profit-sharing plan. They were really pleased. They hadn't expected that. Now everyone feels an ownership in making it a success—because they *are* owners. And the profit-sharing plan also turns out to have tax and retirement advantages for me.

"Just as important, I just got back from ten days in Vail with my family. That shows that the team I've got can get along without me for a few days."

This entrepreneur has created a life he enjoys. He works hard, but he says: "I don't have to look over my shoulder to see what some committee thinks of every move. There's a great pleasure in being your own boss. I get up early each morning, and drive in to work [it's only about twenty minutes away] with a smile on my face."

He doesn't have any worldwide or dramatic growth plans or needs beyond what it takes to give him and his family a good lifestyle. "I want to educate my kids—which costs a lot these days. And we've bought a nice home I've just paid for. And we can now go on some good trips. And I'd like to build up a good stake for my retirement. Maybe I'll sell out in ten years. But in the meantime—I'm enjoying every day. If I grow by five or ten percent a year and keep our existing clients happy, that's fine with me."

Reasonable goals can lead to fulfilling, balanced lifestyles. A definition of success can be as different as every *individual* entrepreneur.

What is your definition of success? Can you create a mission statement that is a reflection of your personal and business goals in two sentences or less?

This would be a good time to try to do a mission statement of your own. To help you with this exercise, we have developed a series of key questions you should consider in creating such a mission statement.

Developing a Mission Statement of Your Own

Now that you've read examples of a variety of mission statements, from large companies that focus more on business objectives to entrepreneurial firms that frequently *balance* business and personal objectives, it's time to prepare your own.

You have to decide, *before* you begin your business, what is your personal definition of success. This becomes part of your mission statement and will help you focus as your business grows. Naturally, any mission statement should be arrived at by listening to your own "intelligent emotions," which will help you in selecting a mission you are comfortable with for your business. And entrepreneurs have also found it useful to discuss any possible mission statement with their spouses or partners. Such feedback can be valuable as a reality check and provide you support when you actually implement your plan. In the meantime, here are some questions to get you started:

1. Have you selected a business you really love?
2. Have you decided to be a small business or a big business?
3. Have you thought about what it means to get big and then be forced to give up doing what you love?
4. If you choose to be a big business, are you willing to work an 80-hour week with no vacations for years if that is what it takes to succeed?
5. Does being the best in your field appeal to you—even if that means you are not the biggest?
6. Can you stay small and resist the temptation to increase overhead? Would you feel comfortable with such a decision? Do you understand the danger of getting caught in the middle?
7. Have you evaluated what kind of lifestyle you want out of your business in terms of the number of hours a week you're going to work, the number of vacations you want, and the amount of money you expect to make out of your business?
8. Can you live with this lifestyle for the foreseeable future?
9. Do you have a realistic timetable for your financial expectations so that you will not be living and working without really knowing how well you are doing?
10. Can you write down your mission statement in one or two sentences? Do these sentences clearly capture your perso-

nal and your business ambitions? Are they bold enough to excite you?

11. Are you ready to put down a specific business plan or road map as the next step in achieving your mission? If so, you are ready to go onto our next chapter, which spells out the importance of consistently following that road map.

Detours to Disaster

"Opportunistic shortcuts that seem like a good idea at the time can bring your business to a place you never, ever thought you'd be."

—An entrepreneur who set up his business in a place where it was bound to fail

Now that you have completed step 1 of your planning process by defining your mission statement and writing it down in one or two sentences, step 2 is to develop your road map. Without a detailed road map, it is easy for you to take a detour to disaster—no matter whether your original mission statement was to build a world-class software organization or bake the best bread in Boston.

The very act of writing down a plan and establishing your road map—it can be done in as few as two or three pages—will help you clarify your direction and stay on track.

The more focused and more detailed the road map, the better the trip and the more success you will have in reaching your planned destination. The business world rewards those who stick to a plan. But the biggest challenge many entrepreneurs face is the temptation to go off-track. Before you write your own road map, let us explain what we have personally experienced and heard from many of the entrepreneurs we interviewed. Here are some examples of detours to disaster. Understanding these potential dangers will help you prepare your business plan and stick to it.

A detour to disaster can come disguised as an ideal shortcut. But don't be fooled. Three classic signs that you are about to be tempted to take a detour are:

- It looks like a shortcut to easy riches.
- You are given the illusion you can do it without an expenditure of a lot of your own time.
- It is an area you know little if nothing about.

Taking such a detour is like heading for the bright lights of New York and ending up on the dangerous streets of Newark—a place you never, ever wanted to be. You had a clear mission statement of where you wanted to go, but—somehow—you took a small "shortcut" and minutes later you are hopelessly lost and even farther from your original destination.

And yet when you are first starting out as an entrepreneur, a detour is awfully hard to resist. When you are first struggling to make your business a success, you are particularly vulnerable. This is when the devil of detours appears—to whisper in your ear how easy it would be to leave your road map for just a quick opportunity. Your desperation makes you prey to the temptation of just a "little" detour.

Like a detour that Sheila and her partner took—that landed them so far off track they almost lost their business.

The Big Money Temptation

In leaving their corporate life, where they were high-ranking executives in large multinational organizations, Sheila and her partner decided to start a business of their own, positioning themselves as consultants to those companies who wished to enter international markets.

Their very first customer, a large American food company, asked them to help focus on Eastern Europe.

Then this organization offered them what turned out to be a detour to disaster: it made a specific request that Sheila and her partner help the company set up a *distribution network* so that the company's canned food could be delivered in stores throughout Poland.

Sheila and her partner had planned to be *consultants,* and yet now they were offered a chance to set up a distribution network for a major customer. They moved forward because there seemed to be no competition in the distribution business. And there was a chance of really big money—many times anything they could earn as consultants. If they could become the major distributors in Poland, they could make millions of dollars.

They were able to convince themselves that this new direction was a good idea. They took this detour—investing their own money in trucks and a support staff to help them deliver the food. They ended up owning over forty trucks, with a staff of 150 people—scattered throughout offices in Poland.

"Have you ever tried to control deliveries to over eight hundred stores when you're sitting in an office in New York?" Sheila asks.

Sheila and her partner finally sold the distribution business after investing much time and effort and without making the fortune they had hoped for.

Sheila says, "I made a mistake in agreeing to go so far from our original mission of being international consultants. As a marketing consultant, I knew about distribution, but in a theoretical way. I didn't know anything about actually running an operation to distribute product—anywhere. Let alone in Poland. If I have one piece of advice for anyone starting out: Think twice before you take a turn that could lead you to a place you never wanted to go—even if you are encouraged to do so by your own customers. I was too tempted by the idea of making a quick fortune."

Today, Sheila says, "I took the detour because I did not have a clear enough road map of where I wanted to go. I set up a marketing consultancy to help companies internationally, with a mission statement of being "great companies' global link." But I had no detailed plan of exactly *how* I was to accomplish that. In retrospect, building a distribution network in Poland could never have been part of my road map."

The lesson here: a mission statement without a road map is an invitation to take a disastrous detour. And the road map should be as detailed as a regular map—with specific locations listed.

In fact, the location you choose can—unless you are careful—also be a detour to disaster.

A Tempting Detour to a Scenic Rather Than a Smart Business Location

Your mission statement is your personal and professional goal. Your road map is the route you will take to reach your goal. A mission statement without a road map can lead you astray, as with one entrepreneur we talked to, who wanted to start a telephone polling operation. His mission statement was "to create a major political polling organization."

He had an excellent background in the business, having worked in exactly the same kind of area for a major company. He had promises from several large customers to use his services. And he planned to open his business in the big city where he had spent his business and personal life and had acquired all his contacts and his expertise.

But then—even before he opened his doors—he took a detour. He was approached by a real estate agent with an offer to locate his offices in a small, scenic town in the country. It was a great real estate deal, and, in thinking it over, it seemed like it would be a wonderful chance for his family to leave the big city behind. Although he was a native New Yorker, like many denizens of that city he had a romantic view of country life. He wanted to give his kids the chance to play out in the fresh country air.

He took the scenic detour, one that he had never planned. He and his family had a good life in the country. But his business faltered. It took him more than a year to realize why. Because he knew the business so well he never prepared a written road map, which might have warned him that he was going down the wrong path.

Political polling is an extremely difficult job, and there is a high rate of burnout. Making countless telephone calls to people who are often in no mood to receive them is not a rewarding long-term experience. It is normal for your basic workforce—the people who actually have to make the calls—to be replaced every three to six months.

It is a good job for the young—with flexible hours and reasonably good money. It is easy to find young people who are going to college and eager to earn a little extra money in cities with great universities. These hungry students are ideal pollsters—able to follow the exacting scripts and not be too depressed by the large percentage of turndowns, a regular feature in such a setup. In large cities, there are also always new batches of college kids coming through, so the high turnover is no problem.

But this entrepreneur moved to a small country town where the workforce was severely limited. Many of the people had a hard time following the scripts. When many of the original workforce left, it was hard to find others. And those who stayed became unhappy employees. They were there because they couldn't find any other work. And more and more, they disliked making the phone calls. Their unhappiness was, naturally enough, communicated over the telephone.

He watched as his business slowly lost customers. In order to save his business he gave up his scenic detour to a small country town and returned to the big city.

The lesson here is that when you are tempted by the wrong location, remember: Once you have a clear, achievable mission statement, it is wise to make sure that you have a road map that leads *directly* to your destination.

When "Can Do!" Can Cripple You

Mike took an equally opportunistic detour, with equally unfortunate results. He had started a company that offered clients marketing advice. His mission statement was "to be known as the marketing company that can solve the impossible problem." One of his first clients was an NFL football team that hired him to help solve their major marketing problems.

It was a great assignment, and he threw himself into it. He came back with an analysis of what was wrong and a series of action steps that he recommended. His study was reviewed by the manager of the team, and he was given approval to implement it.

Moving from consultant to implementer is a detour you should be aware of. Once you become responsible for actually implementing your ideas, you come very close to being an employee rather than an objective observer. You can also become involved in areas that have nothing to do with your original road map, and that's just what happened to Mike.

Yet Mike responded with an enthusiastic "Can do!" and was soon on a detour to disaster.

He began the difficult job of implementing many of his ideas in the marketing area of the organization. The further he got into it, the more he realized that the team needed a full-time marketing director. This was not a job he himself aspired to—he had just left a major company to have his own business, and he did not want to go back to being an organization man for anybody. So he proposed to the manager of the team that they look outside for someone with the proper qualifications to be the marketing director of the organization.

The manager agreed and asked him to handle the search for a new person.

Mike took on this assignment as well, little realizing at the time that this detour would land him in the role of *headhunter.*

For the next two months, in addition to building his consultancy with other clients and trying to implement his ideas for the NFL team, Mike spent an incredible amount of time he could barely spare interviewing people for the job of marketing director.

Finally he was able to find a good candidate. But after he introduced his candidate into the organization, he discovered that the job was not a good opportunity—for anyone. The manager of the team had decided to move the franchise. He had also decided to make a "clean break" with the past—including any recent hires. While Mike could not disagree with his idea (the manager proved that a fresh start was just what was needed to make the team a success), he realized that a lot of his efforts—especially in the personnel area—had been wasted. Mike, who had started life as a successful consultant, ended just six months later as an unsuccessful headhunter. During that time he had to turn down many more profitable opportunities. His enthusiastic, opportunistic "Can do!" detour cost him financially and professionally.

Tip to avoid temptation: Don't say "Can do!" when you have no road map and no idea where "Can do!" can take you.

Avoid a Detour to a Business World You Know Nothing About

A common problem is that many start with the idea of having their own business, yet do not have a clear mission statement about what specifically they want to achieve. The result is often a detour to a field they were never in before, without having a chance to really understand what they are getting into. (The discipline of writing the mission statement can help avoid such a detour.)

John Coe worked for Anaconda Copper for twenty years. He rose up the executive ranks and was well rewarded. But, like so many employees, he dreamed of becoming an entrepreneur. He wanted to have his own business.

He was able to save enough to have some capital to invest, so he made a careful study of the possibilities of buying a business. He wanted to invest in a business that was already doing well—one that had a well-established reputation.

He found a company that made boilers, located in Los Angeles. It was called Rite Engineering. After further investigation, he bought it. Having helped lead a major business like Anaconda Copper, he felt he was prepared and capable of handling a small business like Rite Engineering.

Upon his purchase, the original owner left—and left John Coe with a whole host of problems that he was unprepared to handle. Problems he had a hard time learning how to solve. For making boilers was a whole new world for Coe. It was a complete detour from anything he had ever done before.

"It took me four years to really understand the business and begin to turn it around. By that time we were close to failing. Because of my inexperience in the business, I trusted people to make decisions that I should have made. I barely made it."

A detour to disaster can come disguised as a good business investment. But check—yourself—to make sure you are experienced enough in the field to handle the business when you become the key player.

As an owner you will be expected—required—to make decisions about virtually every aspect of the business you become involved in. Those decisions are difficult if not impossible to make if you don't have previous knowledge to draw upon.

John Coe was fortunate. Through great strength of character and some unusual business strategies—which we discuss later—he was able to make a success of his entrepreneurial venture.

John's success is rare in our research on entrepreneurs. Most fail when they take a detour into areas they know nothing about. John had a mission to become an entrepreneur, but he went out without a road map and almost lost his way.

You don't have to live so dangerously.

Role Models Can Be Very Helpful in Showing You Which Way to Go

In putting your own business plan or road map together, it is sometimes helpful to look for role models—people or companies who have gone down a similar road. Maybe you can follow their lead.

That was the strategy followed by entrepreneurs Bill Backer and Carl Spielvogel, whom we have introduced before, when they left their jobs at a major communications conglomerate to found their own advertising agency.

"We wanted to have our own shop," Bill Backer says. "Not too big. With about a dozen clients we really liked. Clients we could do good work for.

"Carl and I looked around for a role model for just that kind of agency. William Esty seemed like that kind of operation. They had a few, great clients and they had built a great agency with only one office. We took them as our role model." Backer & Spielvogel became one of the most successful advertising agencies in America—in record time. They were able to achieve this speedy progress at least in part by following a role model in the business.

Good role models of business success can exist in almost every field. It is wise to see what those early leaders have done and what you can learn in modeling your road map on theirs. Sometimes going down a proven track is better than trying to make it up as you go along.

A Good Road Map Can Help You Make Sure That Friends Don't Lead You Astray, Especially When You Are Just Starting Out

Dilys Evans is now the proud owner and operator of a business she has built.

Her mission statement could have been defined as "Building a business that celebrates the fine art of children's book illustration."

Her business plan or road map was equally simple and original: she would become an agent and manager representing only those children's book artists she believed were truly exceptional. And she would only represent a certain number—so that she could really devote herself to helping them create wonderful books. She named her business Dilys Evans Fine Illustration.

Dilys had her greatest temptations when she first started out.

"I was eager to get the first published books in my hands," she says, "and I had many opportunities to represent people who were not as talented as I was looking for. Some of my good friends in the business were encouraging me to lower my standards. They told me I should go for high volume by representing more artists even if their work wasn't as good as I demanded, and I would have a bigger business. I didn't agree. I felt I must start by representing the very best, and become known that way.

"I stuck to my plan. I had a few lean months, but gradually the quality of the artists I represented became known. I had created my own place in the market and I became known as someone you could count on to deliver work of truly exceptional quality.

"I believe that if I had taken that detour away from my plan to represent the very best talent, I would *never* have been able to build the successful business I have today. Now I'm asked to curate major art shows throughout the country featuring the fine art of children's book illustration. It took some courage to stay on course—but the results have been worth it."

Dilys Evans is an excellent example of the importance of staying true to your personal and professional mission statement, and on track with your own road map, despite all opportunistic temptations.

A Road Map Can Give You a Competitive Edge

Phil Knight, founder of Nike, is a good example of an entrepreneur who planned for his success.

Twenty-five years ago Adidas made the best-selling running shoes in America, and in the rest of the world. Adidas's distinctive two-stripe logo was on the running shoes of most of the world's greatest athletes.

Phil Knight was envious of Adidas, and also impatient with them. He thought they could be beaten—that their virtual monopoly of the running shoe market could be overthrown.

Phil had always loved running. His personal and professional mission could be said to be to build a successful business in running shoes. Such a mission statement would combine his love for running with making money. His goal was to be as successful as Adidas. Such a goal seemed impossible at the time.

But Knight developed a unique *business plan* to achieve his mission. While he was at Stanford Business School, he put together a study that showed it would be feasible to beat Adidas by manufacturing running shoes that were just as good if not better, but producing them in Asia, where the costs of production would be much lower. Adidas is a German company, with relatively high built-in overhead.

Knight followed his plan.

He founded Nike, a company based on the premise put down in his business plan. He designed excellent running shoes and then had them built in Asia, where the production costs were much less.

He sold these shoes in America and was able to gain market share, because their quality was as good if not better than Adidas, yet he was able to sell them for less.

Phil Knight was able to get Nike off the ground because he followed not only his mission of becoming involved in running, but his *business plan* of how to do so in a profitable way. He had a clear road map to help him in his journey toward building a successful business.

A Road Map Can Help
You Manage Change

"I'm always planning for what might happen tomorrow," Jerry Mink, M.D., whom we met before, says, "because if you don't, you might not make it.

"I decided when I was about twelve I wanted to be a doctor," Dr. Mink says, "but today even a doctor has to do more than just have a practice—he's got to have some plan. Particularly with the rapid changes occurring in the field of medicine these days."

Dr. Mink, a published authority on radiology, says: "I have three keys to all my plans: (1) I want to be and to work with the greatest doctors, (2) I want to work with the greatest technology (and that is changing all the time), and (3) I want to work with the greatest hospitals.

"My partners and I have unequaled credentials in our field. We really know what we are doing in radiology. Recently we teamed up with a company that is going to give us the resources we need to continue to purchase the latest and best technology for radiology. And we have also built up excellent relationships with several great hospitals in our area. In the old days, a doctor had to physically *be* at the hospital. Now, with our advanced, digitalized technology we can analyze many X rays almost as fast as they are being taken—wherever they are. For the hospitals it means they get medical opinions from the leading experts in the field. For us, it means we have a chance to share our expertise more effectively. And we aren't dependent on any one hospital for our future."

Using his ability to successfully plan for the future, Dr. Mink has built the most respected radiology operation on the West Coast.

A Unique Road Map—Backed by Unique Strength of Character— Is the Best Way to Get a New Idea off the Ground

Fred Smith, founder of Federal Express, wrote a plan for a business while he was still an undergraduate at Yale. He loved to fly, and his mission was to develop a business built around flying. He developed a business plan, or road map, that was based on a *new idea.* He described a business that was founded on the concept of delivering the mail by using a hub in which everything would come into a central airport, and then be distributed across the country. Smith thought that his hub-and-spokes theory could offer economies of scale and be more efficient than any present system for delivering packages.

His professor at Yale judged that this business plan was worthy of a C.

After Smith got out of Yale and returned from several tours to Vietnam, he followed his mission, implemented his road map, and created Federal Express.

Though it wasn't easy to get his business off the ground, by persistently following his road map, by never giving up on his original idea, Fred Smith was able to win in the end. He built a hub at the Memphis airport, and was able to get the mail turned around and back out more effectively than most of his competitors.

Today, Federal Express has expanded on this basic hub-and-spokes theory with other hubs in America and around the world. Federal Express is now the leader in overnight deliveries.

But the key ingredient in implementing his plan was Fred Smith's amazing courage and strength of character. If he had not persisted—against all odds—the plan would have been a failure.

This strength of character—embodied in the inspiring story of Fred Smith's creation of Federal Express—is what distinguishes the great entrepreneurs from those who simply dream of being.

To turn an original idea into a dynamic reality takes an effort that can be sustained only if you have the strength of character to keep going when all others doubt you. And part of the necessary leadership of all of the most successful entrepreneurs is to inspire others to exceed the boundaries of what they thought they were capable of achieving.

Fred Smith not only created a unique hub-and-spokes system, he also created a unique organization that delivered a level of excellence and service never seen before.

To achieve his dream, Fred Smith had to have great strength of character and had to communicate that strength in an inspiring way to everyone involved in getting his new idea off the ground.

Making a road map and having the strength of character to implement it, despite all odds, can help *your* dreams come true.

A Road Map Can Give You the Discipline to Stick to Your Plan

Tom Margittai says that one his biggest challenges was "resisting the boredom of sticking to my plan."

He says that he had been offered the chance to franchise his restaurants around the world. Not once, but many times.

"People," Tom says, "came to me and told me how much richer I could be by franchising my restaurant. But I resisted that idea.

"I realized that I would lose quality control with all that franchising. And I reminded myself that I wanted to create a great restaurant in New York—not go running around the world pretending to be some empire builder."

Tom Margittai successfully resisted the temptation to take a major detour from his original dream.

Now it is time for us to do an exercise with you to begin to develop *your* own road map.

Designing an Effective Road Map

Your road map is your *how*—how you will achieve your mission. Your mission can be a variety of different possible destinations: from becoming the world's top software creator to baking the best bread in Boston. Your mission is *what* you want to do. Your road map is *how* you will do it.

In coming up with a one- or two-sentence definition of your mission, you asked yourself what you loved to do. And if you wanted to be big or a smaller size you could control.

In coming up with your road map, *you must ask realistic questions of how to plan to make your dream come true.*

Many major Fortune 500 companies have found that using a particular technique helps them understand the realities they might face with a new product or entry in today's crowded marketplace. That technique is called SWOT.

SWOT is an acronym that stands for strengths, weaknesses, opportunities, and threats.

When you are creating a road map it is helpful to go through a SWOT process, for your dream is like a new product or service in an already crowded marketplace. We will give you an example of a SWOT experience in the next chapter, but there are some questions you can ask yourself right now. These questions are for you and for your business idea.

What are your strengths? What are the strengths of the idea? What are your weaknesses? What could be the weaknesses of what you want to do? What are the opportunities you see out there that give you confidence you will succeed? What are the threats? What competition, for example, can you expect (even if it doesn't exist right now)?

To answer the questions and go through SWOT properly, you will have to do research. Often a lot of research. You should read as much as you can about the field you plan to enter. You should find any case histories of similar business operations. Libraries and colleges can be extremely helpful in this research phase of the SWOT process.

Next, you should go out into the marketplace and talk to people who have tried something similar to your mission. Role models, as we have discussed, can be invaluable in helping you prepare your own road map.

After all your research is done, see if you can put down in two or three pages *how* you plan to achieve your dream.

It is the experience of most entrepreneurs that the simpler your road map, the more sure you are of reaching your destination.

Remember: you cannot successfully pursue two business objectives at once, and you should not have too many strategies or roads to your objective. In other words, if you can't clearly describe the road you wish to take to your business destination, then don't take it. You will only get lost.

Before you complete your road map, you should establish specific markers that will tell you whether you are making progress. You should have actual financial goals and realistic times when you expect to achieve them. You can create your own *speedometer*—which will be your predetermined measure that will help to tell you whether or not you are proceeding along your road map with the speed and success you originally imagined. Your speedometer can be based on revenues you have brought in, profits after tax, or any other measurement device you choose.

The importance of this process is to choose some *objective* measurement with which you can judge your speed. (Your friendly accountant will be invaluable here.)

Then you will have a sense of progress and a better understanding of how well you are doing. Entrepreneurs have found that it is a lot easier to get somewhere if they have taken the time to establish a way of measuring their progress before they begin their journey.

The Importance of Test-Marketing Your Business Plan—Before You Leave

Now that you've developed your mission statement and road map, you can test-market them before you start your own business or leave your job.

As Bill Backer said to us: "I always think it's best, if you're a new entrepreneur, to check out your idea first to see if you like it. Otherwise, you might find yourself dreaming of going to the North Pole, and yet when you finally actually get there you might find yourself saying that you don't like it there because it's just too damn *cold*."

Some inexperienced entrepreneurs find themselves at the North Pole, or other places they didn't really want to be, because they didn't give themselves a chance to experience what the business was really like *before* they got into it.

What many don't realize is that there is almost always a way to try it to see if you like it.

An entrepreneurial couple we talked to had always wanted to run a bed-and-breakfast.

He was an executive in a Fortune 500 company. She was an

administrator in the local school system. Their children were grown, and they were looking for something new to do.

They saved themselves from a terrible misadventure by testing their dream—before they tried to live it.

They decided to spend one vacation actually working in a bed-and-breakfast. They found owners of a bed-and-breakfast that were happy to have their help for a two-week period.

The first morning everything went well. He enjoyed talking with the guests; he even enjoyed helping prepare the breakfast. She also liked acting as a kind of hostess during that first day.

But things went downhill as the days went by—and the drudgery in much of the work took its toll. She didn't enjoy changing the sheets on the beds that much, and he definitely didn't like the job of fixing the plumbing. In fact, he discovered that he was quite bad at fixing things around the house—which turned out to be an essential job. She discovered that she didn't really enjoy doing housework all day.

They were good sports—they kept going throughout the two weeks. But, by the end, they were treating it more like a challenge in survival than a possible personal and professional lifestyle for themselves. The joy had gone out of their dream as they really got to experience it.

By the end of their "vacation," they had decided that running a bed-and-breakfast was not a fantasy for them—the brief taste of reality had convinced them of that. And they felt very fortunate that they had had a chance to experience what running and working at a bed-and-breakfast was really like—before they had to go out on their own.

Think of all the money and time and agony they avoided by test-marketing their idea! You never really know whether you are going to be good at something until you try it. Unless you try it, you won't even know whether you really *like* it.

Another entrepreneur had an opposite experience, in the sense that he discovered, through trying something new, that he was really good at it and really enjoyed doing it. His name is Bob Klimecki. Bob was a furniture designer. And very successful. One of his top clients was a real estate owner who asked Bob to design the interiors of the furnished apartments he was renting.

Almost by accident, Bob discovered that by having tasteful furnishings in apartments, they were easier to rent. In other words, when people rented furnished apartments, they were influenced by the style of the interiors.

This gave Bob an idea. He decided to start getting into the business of renting furnished apartments. He thought that he could do the furnishings better than the competition, and thus be successful.

Bob bought a small apartment building and tried out his idea (while at the same time maintaining his original job). Bob was extremely successful in his real estate venture. He also discovered that he enjoyed the business.

Today, he has built a successful real estate business for himself. And it all started with a successful test-market of his original idea while he was still employed.

Lesson: Whether or not you enjoy it, you will always learn from your test-market. It is a low-risk, high-reward chance for you to see if your road map works. So, if possible, always test-market your road map—before you leave on the trip of a lifetime. As much as possible, talk to people already in the business, spend time in the business, even be willing to spend a vacation working for free in the business you plan to get into, and see if you like it—before you go out and set up *your* own business.

Summation

Successful entrepreneurs *plan* to make their dreams come true. They follow a proven, three-step process:

1. Develop a *mission statement* of two sentences or less that clearly defines your definition of personal and business success. This is *what* you want to do. This will now be your desired destination.
2. Complete a *road map* of two or three pages that focuses on a single business objective and includes specific strategies of exactly how you are going to get to your destination. This is the how-to, practical guide that will help you avoid opportunistic detours and stay on track. Your road map should include objective signs of success along the way that can act as a kind of speedometer to assure you that you are getting to your destination and achieving your mission as quickly as you planned. If possible, you should test-market this road map to make sure it matches your expectations.
3. Finally, *understand yourself*—your strengths and weaknesses and how your business can be seen as *unique*—for, in the final analysis, as an entrepreneur this will be the single most important factor in making your plan a success. You must not only design a road map, you must also be the car that travels that road, *stands out* from the competition, and is *unique enough* to attract the business.

What kind of car are you? A BMW? A Chevy? A Jeep? What kind of personality do you have that will help to distinguish you from all others traveling down similar roads hoping to achieve equal success?

In the competitive marketing world of today, it is no longer enough to simply have a clear mission statement and an excellent road map. For your dream to come true, and for you to reap the rewards and recognition you deserve, you also need a unique marketing promise: *You've got to be a brand.* A brand that is built on some unique selling proposition, or USP.

Our next chapter will help you understand how to become the unique brand with the USP you need to succeed.

Fired Up! Fired Up! Fired Up! Fired Up! Fired Up! Fired Up! Fired Up! Fired Up! Fired Up! Fired Up! Fired Up!

164

You've Got to Be a Brand

"**I** didn't think I'd have to market my restaurant the way you sell a box of Tide—but today it's the only way to build a business."

—David Davis, successful entrepreneur and owner of the Pub Restaurant in Norfolk, Connecticut

It is eleven-thirty A.M. at the headquarters of the big company you presently work for. You are, as usual, in a meeting—a meeting you were specifically told by your boss was "too important to miss." You look around the room and see at least thirty of your peers.

The speaker has already droned on for the last hour, and you now notice, with a sinking heart, that he has a large stack of slides still to go through. He is too boring to believe, yet too senior to confront—if you value your job.

He is your worst corporate nightmare: the Vampire Presenter. A Vampire Presenter is one who drinks the lifeblood of his audience to keep him going. He is able to leave his audience mentally lifeless.

In good corporate meeting style, your eyes remain open (it is bad form to be seen to sleep), fixed, apparently on the slides, but secretly you start to think about other things—anything—to maintain your brain.

You realize that you are hungry. Breakfast—a single cup of coffee and half a bagel—seems like another lifetime ago.

You remember the great dinner you had last night. You had gone with friends to a wonderful new restaurant. You were greeted at the door and ushered into a charming room. The food was delicious, and the owner came over during the meal to make sure everything was okay. You saw the owner as a fortunate person—someone who had created a wonderful job for himself. He had admiration, financial success—yet it was as though he were giving a great party every night.

Now—hungry, yet trapped in an endless meeting—you begin to dream about owning a restaurant yourself. It is an idea you have played with from time to time. And today it takes on much more irresistible allure. The more bored and hungry you become, the more the thought of owning a restaurant seems like the ideal way to get out of the corporate zoo.

What you are now doing—a form of corporate meeting-dreaming—is very normal, and very popular. The corporate meeting is a common incubator for such dreams. In fact, we have found an amazing number of *similar* dreams of what people would like to do when they leave the corporate zoo. From owning a restaurant to having an antique store to becoming a photographer—if you have dreams such as these, you are not alone. Yet many of these people proceed beyond the dreaming stage.

The issue then becomes: How do you make *your* dream come true? In our judgment, what distinguishes the successful entrepreneurs from those who barely survive is their ability to carve out a distinctive niche by becoming a unique brand.

A viable mission statement, a good road map, and being a brand with a powerful unique selling proposition are the three key ingredients in the plan of successful entrepreneurs. To develop your business to the highest potential, you will need to create a way to separate yourself from the competition by becoming such a unique brand.

You need to communicate the benefits you plan to offer potential customers in such a way that your business *stands out* from the crowd.

Remember all those *similar* dreams? Successful entrepreneurs find a way to make their dreams into *unique* realities. That is what building a unique brand is all about.

What Is a Unique Brand?

A unique brand is an original combination of a name, a graphic look, what the product or service does and a personality that all come together to communicate a benefit to your potential customers.

In the advertising business, this benefit has become known as a unique selling proposition, or USP. (This phrase was coined by Rosser Reeves about thirty years ago when he was working for Ted Bates Advertising. He wrote a book about the power of USP that helped to popularize the concept. The book is still in print today.)

A USP is something relevant and original that can be claimed for a particular product or service. The USP should be able to communicate: Buy our brand and get this unique benefit.

Many major companies employ a powerful USP to build their business, as do *most successful entrepreneurs*. While the entrepreneurs might not call it that or realize it, they also use a key distinctive marketing approach to distinguish themselves from their competition. As an entrepreneur, you will need to develop your own USP. A USP is not a luxury—it is a necessity.

There are many famous examples of successful USPs, used to build unique brands:

- M&M'S—"THE MILK CHOCOLATE MELTS IN YOUR MOUTH, NOT IN YOUR HAND."®
- Visa—"We Are Everywhere You Want to Be."
- Federal Express—"When it absolutely, positively has to be there overnight."

On a much smaller scale, we know of a roofing company that uses a name to make itself a unique brand: Reliable Roofing. What could be a better name for such a company, and who could have a more powerful or relevant USP?

A small local bank we know advertises that it offers "Personal service that is safe, sound and secure." That combination of personal service with security is also an excellent USP.

The important point is that your USP should help to make your brand of business *stand out* from the crowd in a positive way.

In the big business of the 1990s there is a direct correlation between the best-*known* brands and the best-selling brands. In every product category. This will also be true of your business—whatever its size. You have to become known for offering some unique reason why you deserve to be in business—or you won't be in business long.

It is no longer enough to build a better mousetrap and wait for the world to beat a path to your door. Today you have to develop a unique brand by marketing the unique benefits of the better mousetrap with a powerful USP, or the world will never know.

You might be thinking: "I'm not going to try to sell candy or credit cards with fancy TV commercials, an overnight delivery service, or even a roofing service or a bank. I've got such a little business to launch that I don't need to be a unique brand with a powerful USP."

Surprise: Your Business Is Already a Brand. The Real Question Becomes: Are You a Unique Brand?

Just as surely as the ranchers branded their cattle, your new business has probably already given itself *some* brand identity.

Even before your new baby of a business is born, you have probably thought about what would be the right name. And you might already have a *name,* a *business card, stationery.* These are the building blocks of your brand identity.

For brands are not simply something created by major companies in TV commercials, but by every entrepreneur, whatever the size or scale of his or her business. A storefront sign or a business card are some of the most powerful branding devices around. The real question becomes not whether or not your business is going to be a brand (you already are), but rather whether you are going to be a *unique* brand that has a powerful enough USP to succeed.

Any money you spend going into a business will be wasted if you haven't developed a unique brand with a powerful-enough USP to help you stand out among the competition and attract the kind of customers you want. Even putting up a sign with your company name will be wasted—if it is not the correct competitive position for the market. It might even turn people off.

On the other hand, any money you spend on marketing will be multiplied many times over if you have come up with a unique brand identity.

Why Successful Entrepreneurs Must Be Unique Brands

Most new business efforts fail. They are lost from sight in the crowded marketplace. To us, coming from marketing backgrounds, this is a terrible waste of talent and effort. Yet many would-be entrepreneurs are often shocked when they discover the importance marketing has assumed—in building any new business.

Today, powerful, targeted marketing is just as *essential* as any other dimension in assuring entrepreneurial success. And all of marketing is targeted at one vital objective: becoming a unique brand.

There are three, key reasons entrepreneurs have got to be a unique brand. It's as simple as one, two, three:

1. Parity is simply the price of admission to any business today. People expect—even demand—a certain basic level of service and product excellence. You've got to add a *parity plus*—the reason people in a crowded marketplace will chose to buy from *you*. The *plus* is the unique benefit that can distinguish you from the rest. Even a business as basic as a restaurant simply offering food to people needs to distinguish itself from all those other restaurants already well established with a host of loyal customers.

2. Virtually any field you are going into today is already crowded and extremely competitive. Even if *you* believe that your business is unique, you will quickly discover there are others with similar ideas—going after some of the same customers. You've got to find a way to be noticed. You'd better have a unique brand with a relevant and original USP or you will not be

able to receive the notice you deserve. It could be as simple as what your competition could also claim, but doesn't. If you claim it, then you have preempted their ability to do so. Many new businesses sink from sight before they have really had a chance to grow because they were not launched as a unique brand with a powerful, attention-getting USP.

3. In a marketing phrase, you get more "bang for the buck" if you launch your entrepreneurial venture as a unique brand from the very beginning. When you do it from the start, each piece of communication, from your letterhead to your business card, then builds to gain you increased recognition in a consistent way that builds positive momentum in your favor.

These three reasons apply whatever the size or kind of business you are planning to get into.

Even if you are one of those people who dream about having a restaurant one day, you still face this crucial challenge. In fact, this is exactly what an entrepreneur we talked to faced.

Building a Unique Brand

David Davis was frustrated working in a large organization. "I felt," he says, "that I was spending more time trying to please my boss than taking care of our customers. My biggest frustration in corporate life was spending sixty to seventy percent of my workday telling my boss what a great guy he was, and only a small percentage on my work."

He was also demoralized by the quality of the management at the top of his company. "You realize," he says, "that if you have second-rate people at the top, and they are hiring third-rate people because they are too insecure to do anything else, the future of your company is not very bright. We were imploding from within, doomed to a slow defeat in our market, and the harder I worked to try to change things, the more frustrated I became."

He shared a popular corporate dream: opening a restaurant in some beautiful country town. In fact, he and his wife made that their personal and professional mission.

His mission statement was: "To live and work in a small town in the country."

The road map or business plan to achieve his mission was to take the strategy of owning a restaurant, preferably the only one in a small country town.

In developing his road map, he used the SWOT process, which, as you recall, helps you to focus on four key points: strengths, weaknesses, opportunities, and threats to your business.

As a strength, he noticed that it was the only bar and restaurant in the town. In addition, he thought that the basic decor and interior space needed little change.

A weakness he noted was that the current name—the Hawk's Nest—was definitely unappetizing. There was also no particular unique specialty or claim or personality to the place. It was just another restaurant, without any real distinction, which might partially account for another weakness: a slowly decreasing clientele.

Which led him to a major opportunity: If he could change the name, come up with some more distinctive personality, and encourage new trial by the folks of the town, he was certain he could improve the balance sheet.

Which led him to his major threat: He knew he mustn't do anything, in "improving" the restaurant, to lose his current customers. Losing the existing business was his major threat.

After the SWOT he felt his road map was simple, if challenging: Change the name and come up with some unique specialty or attitude to attract new business, while keeping the still-loyal customers coming back for more.

Coming Up with a Unique Selling Proposition (USP)

David bought the restaurant and then discovered his USP through his customers—which is often the best way to go. When you are looking for a way to stand out from the crowd, sometimes it is wise to let the crowd tell you what they are looking for.

He was talking to some customers one day in the bar of his restaurant—the most important profit center—and they asked him about some exotic beer. He happened to have ordered a case, being quite a knowledgeable beer connoisseur himself. They were very impressed. And came back frequently to talk with him about beer, and sample other brands.

He decided to make his knowledge of beer and the wide variety of beers he offered into a major strength. After doing a bit of research, he discovered that most restaurants offered at most a dozen brands.

Today, he offers 151 different kinds of beer. Which is a perfect support for what became his USP: "The widest selection of the finest beers in the world."

His powerful USP attracted a lot of publicity—invaluable for building his business.

He got a photograph of himself and his restaurant on the front page of the local newspaper. A regional magazine did a story about him, and his great selection of the finest beers—which was literally unheard of in that corner of New England. Even the *New York Times* was enticed to have a top food critic visit his premises, and he got a great review.

All the recognition occurred because he spent the time to make his restaurant unique with a powerful, relevant USP.

The previous owners had never received any publicity.

Make Sure You Have the Best Name for Your USP

Now that David had his USP, it was much easier to decide on the right name. The Hawk's Nest obviously conveyed nothing about beer, or even food—unless you were into eating a hawk or a nest—so he decided to change the name to: the Pub.

The Pub sounds like a place that might have a good selection of excellent beer. And he felt comfortable with the name, for he was English. Which leads to our next point . . .

Make Sure Your Personality Is Consistent with Your USP

The personality of the founder or the owner of any business casts a long shadow.

That means that whatever unique position you decide to carve out for yourself in the marketplace, you must feel comfortable in reinforcing that position with your own personality.

David felt completely comfortable in the role as owner/host of a local pub in a small country town. This was, indeed, the realization of his personal and professional mission.

His happiness in his role reinforced his USP and his name and gave his budding brand more recognition and ever greater success.

Your Packaging Must Reflect Your USP and Your Personality

The physical appearance of your business or your product or service has got to be congruent with your USP.

In the case of the Pub, he put up a new "publike" sign out front. He offered a few more English-sounding items to the menu.

And that was enough, in addition to his own English accent and rather English dress and manner, to give people permission to enjoy the whole unique personality of his business.

In addition, he has a large slate on which he puts up each week the current number of exotic beers he carries. And each week, he crosses out the previous number, as the digits increase.

The slate and the specific and growing number of beers help reinforce his USP.

Be the Brand You Love to Be

The final secret to building a successful brand is choosing a USP and personality that are close to your favorite fantasy. People who love what they are doing are liked by others. We buy from those we like. The business world loves a lover.

David became happier and happier as his creation—his new brand the Pub, with "the widest selection of the finest beers in the world"—increased its business. Nothing is more exciting than seeing your ideas work in the marketplace.

His happiness was contagious.

It not only convinced the current customers to stay, but encouraged new people to come back for more. Today, the Pub is doing more business than ever before.

He turned his favorite, if common dream into an uncommon

and successful reality. And he did it by marketing properly—by making sure he offered the market something more, something that could brand his business as unique.

In the restaurant business, it is simply the price of admission to offer good food and drink in a good location. Our friend knew he needed a unique brand with a powerful USP, a new name, and a personality he could feel comfortable with.

"You have to spend time with a lot of lawyers and accountants in any business," David Davis says, "but if you don't build a unique brand with a powerful USP, you'll never get the recognition you deserve. The *New York Times* might never have noticed me without the beer gambit."

A Unique Brand with a Powerful USP Can Turn Your Dream into a Successful Reality—No Matter the Size of Your Dream

We've taken you through a common dream that became uncommonly successful—a booming restaurant in a beautiful little country town. But the *same marketing principles* apply to launching a major restaurant in any big city in the world.

When the Four Seasons was launched in New York it became the number-one restaurant in the city in its first year. It had a unique name, and a unique idea: It would change its menu, and even its decor, four times a year.

Though New York can be a city of cynics, no one could resist going to the new restaurant—not once, but four times—to see each new season arrive. The Four Seasons got incredible and sustained trial over a whole year—more than enough time to build loyal fans to help turn the Four Seasons into the unique brand it is today, known for its excellent cuisine presented in an exciting atmosphere where the most powerful people in New York gather to make deals and dine.

Today, the Four Seasons still has a unique approach, although the idea of completely changing the interior decor every four seasons has been discontinued. Now the trees and flowers change with the seasons and the logo simply has the four different seasons dramatized by four different trees.

McDonald's is, of course, yet another example of someone in the restaurant business who put together a unique brand—at the opposite end of the scale.

The golden arches, the original sign digitally recording each sale, plus fast service and low prices, gave McDonald's a preeminent share in a business it helped create: the fast-food hamburger restaurant.

Many Mom and Pop hamburger joints laughed at McDonald's and assumed that their customers would always stay with them. Marketing a unique Brand made McDonald's, and keeps it growing as the *unbranded* hamburger stands disappear.

Becoming a unique brand can be a powerful engine for growth—whatever the size of your business, and whatever business you decide to go into.

From Restaurants to Computers to Old Masters to Pickles—Becoming a Unique Brand Makes Entrepreneurial Dreams Come True

What is true for restaurants is also true for virtually every successful business created by hardworking entrepreneurs. A unique brand with a powerful USP must be carefully created to offer a relevant solution to a perceived consumer need. When that is achieved, success is sure.

And the idea of becoming a unique brand, which works so well for launching a new restaurant, can also work for launching an electronics store. While the *tactics* would obviously be different, the basic strategy would be the same: Develop a memorable name, a unique brand with a compelling USP, and personality.

Cameron Estes is a successful entrepreneur who now runs one of the largest groups of retail stores in the Chicago area specializing in selling the latest electronics.

His company's name, ELEK-TEK, conveys both electronics and technology and a high-quality, high-variety selection. It is also short and easy to remember.

His USP? "The most current computer products from the best national brands at the lowest discounted prices, with great customer support both pre and post sale."

The personality he conveys is one of high energy, high value by offering an excellent selection of the highest-quality products at the lowest prices—all put on display in a uniquely user-friendly environment: with popular music, beautifully displayed computers, and helpful, upbeat sales people. You can imagine how his stores stand out from those of his competitors—which tend to be cold and warehouse format, with unexplained displays of technology that can be very intimidating.

Visiting an ELEK-TEK store is like going to a toy store for grown-ups. He has captured the excitement and the fun that technology can be. This inviting atmosphere helps those who are threatened by the idea of computers to feel more comfortable. Going to an ELEK-TEK store is an enjoyable experience for everyone.

He has been very successful in clearly standing out in a positive way from his competition. He has built a strong and unique brand with a powerful, relevant USP for his business.

The same marketing principles that work for a chain of electronic stores also work for a single individual.

When Your Name Becomes Your Business Brand

There are many cases when in making your dream into a reality you should stay with your own name; this is especially true if you are launching your business building on your own well-established reputation.

Loretta Barrett, our literary agent, *was* a successful editor at a major publishing company. Yet she still yearned to breathe the empowering air of the entrepreneur. She wanted the freedom of being out on her own.

She thought that she could build a successful business of her own by offering herself as an agent to authors she chose. This role would still give her the opportunity to be a catalyst in getting books published, but would also get her out of what she had come to regard as the claustrophobic corporate culture.

Before she opened her operation, she asked a professional writer to give her some advice about what the name of her business should be. The writer pointed out that the very word *agent* in the title of a business was not a unique asset with either writers or publishers—her two key target groups.

Instead of featuring the word *agent* in the name of her company, it became: Loretta Barrett Books, Inc.

Books were the promise, the goal of her whole business—the end benefit that everyone, publishers and writers alike, was looking for. The name and the benefit made a euphonious whole that has proved to be very successful. Today Loretta Barrett Books is one of the most distinguished literary agencies in the business.

Another example is an entrepreneur who sells Italian old masters: wonderful works in sculpture and painting. These artworks cost a great deal of money. When people give you a lot of money, they like to feel that you are a person of some stature. So he incorporated himself, primarily so that he could say on his business card: Robert Dance, Inc.

He believes that even today—when he is successful and well known to his key clientele—that single word *Inc.* adds a necessary dimension of credibility to his business and gives him his unique brand identity.

What is true for restaurants, electronic stores, and individuals can also be true in marketing pickles.

When John Gray left the world of banking to sell pickles, he kept the company name that was unique, and communicated the taste and the kind of pickles his grandmother used to serve. The name of his business: Bubbies (Pickles) of San Francisco, Inc.

Bubbie is an affectionate Yiddish word for "grandmother." San Francisco is famous for great food. The combination of an original word with a well-known gourmet paradise like San Francisco helped his pickles receive a positive reception.

As he expressed it, he wanted to produce "pickles pickled in the great, old-fashioned way. Pickles that didn't lose their crunch."

The idea behind the brand was put into these words: "Bubbies Pickles of San Francisco. Delicious, crunchy taste because they're made the natural old-fashioned way from Bubbie Rose's secret recipe."

He puts his pickles in an all-natural saltwater brine, without any vinegar, and is careful to make sure they are put in jars and refrigerated properly so that they don't become soft.

"The best pickles have been made the same way for hundreds, even thousands of years," he says. "I just wanted to make sure our customers could still enjoy such quality when you walk into a fancy supermarket today."

Bubbies first became a major brand in the competitive California marketplace and are now eagerly asked for throughout the entire country.

John Childs, whom we introduced earlier, also discovered a company with a unique name and USP. The product was iced tea. Doesn't sound so exciting, does it?

But with a unique name like Snapple, and a USP claiming "Made from the best stuff on earth," the small business from Long Island became a unique brand almost immediately.

When you add a unique brand with a powerful, relevant USP to a clear personal and professional mission and a focused business plan or road map that you follow—without detours—your odds of success dramatically increase.

Here's a checklist to assure your success:

CHECKLIST FOR SUCCESS

1. Do You Have the Best Possible Name?

Research shows that a good name is:

- Short
- Easy to pronounce
- Easy to understand
- Implies a benefit
- Unique
- Memorable

Some examples:

Apple—short, easy to pronounce and understand, and unique. It is also, most importantly, user-friendly. When it was launched in the computer world, it was uniquely warm and human, especially when compared to the cold letters of IBM. And it was memorable. When you heard about an Apple computer, it was impossible to forget.

Apple has also been successful with *Macintosh,* another variety of Apple.

It failed with a brand called Lisa—some say because it didn't have a name that fit with Apple.

Microsoft is a longer name, yet still easy to pronounce, and described the software product perfectly.

Ben & Jerry's ice cream personalized a whole product category. It gave an ice cream the personality of the best of the sixties social philosophy—and a unique entrepreneurial identity in the nineties.

Wouldn't you rather use *Reliable Roofing* than, say, ACME Roofing?

In-A-Bind is the name of a small company offering big companies a chance to get a brochure printed in days—compared to the weeks or even months it normally takes. This simple name has helped break through the clutter of all the other suppliers to build a successful business.

A new food company in Austin, Texas—*Guiltless Gourmet*—has seen the trend towards fat-free foods and branded its salsa and chips with this irresistible name. It is backed by a powerful USP: "Gourmet without the guilt." Guiltless Gourmet is now growing fast—but it was *planned* that way.

An entrepreneur says, "I sometimes think the most important communication in any business is 'Hello, my name is . . . and here's what I can do for you.' If you get your name right, and it implies some benefit, you've got a lot easier job of building a business."

2. Is Your Graphic Approach Clear and Original?
Your graphic approach should relate to your name and build on the unique selling proposition and the benefit it contains.

Examples:

Apple shows an apple, with a bite taken out of it. Once seen, impossible to forget. And, once again, it says human beings are involved, rather than just International Business Machines.

An advertising agency came up with the Rock of Gibraltar as a symbol for Prudential Life Insurance Company almost ninety years ago. The rock is still there. A great graphic never has to die.

Absolut Vodka has used its bottle shape to enter the minds of millions.

And a Ford Mustang, naturally, has always featured a horse on the front of each vehicle it sells.

Recently, John Gray added a visual to his pickle label. "We did some focus groups," John said. "I had been resisting the whole idea of focus groups—when you went out and talked to pickle eaters. I thought I knew enough about eating a pickle without doing any fancy research. I was wrong. The focus groups really helped *me* focus. I realized that I wasn't communicating what is called a unique brand with my original USP as well as I should.

"The focus groups reminded me of the obvious, which is a big asset of that kind of research. It was obvious that most people don't understand that *Bubbie* is Yiddish for 'grandmother.' So we added a picture of a grandmother to our label.

"I thought such a graphic device would have little if any affect on our sales. In the first quarter we used the new label, sales were up by one hundred percent."

3. Can You Say in a Sentence of Ten Words or Less What You Intend to Offer? What Is Your USP?

General Electric sums up all its advertising with the concluding line: "We bring good things to life."

MCI launched an incredibly successful promotion with the words "Friends and family."

We've all heard about "the friendly skies" of United Airlines. And, of course, "Nobody doesn't like Sara Lee."

Snickers has built worldwide business by reminding people: "Packed with Peanuts, SNICKERS Really Satisfies."®

For any entrepreneur, it is critical that you can express your own USP simply. Whether it is a catchy slogan or just a few words telling your potential customers what you do, it is essential for your success that you have some clear, short way of communicating what unique benefit you can offer.

4. Is the Benefit You're Promoting the Most Relevant to Your Customer or Client and the One That Gives You the Biggest Competitive Advantage?

Mercedes-Benz has kept its reputation by reminding prospects that its vehicles are "engineered like no other car in the world."

Nike took over the ownership of encouraging athletic ability by adopting the vernacular phrase "Just do it."

Bloomingdale's has as its slogan "Like no other store in the world," making it a place even Queen Elizabeth must see when she comes to New York.

A dentist we talked to doubled her business when she put a small ad in the local Yellow Pages featuring the promise "Dental gain without the pain."

A dry cleaner in New York who offers excellent quality cleaning at remarkably low prices recently put up this sign in the front window of his store: CLEAN—WITHOUT BEING TAKEN TO THE CLEANERS. It might not be grammatical English, but his USP speaks well enough, and relevantly enough, for him to claim, "I have more customers come in since the sign went up.... More every day."

Arthur Chapman stumbled onto his USP. He was thinking

of leaving life in a big, corporate accounting firm. One of his best friends was a successful Chinese entrepreneur, and he found himself spending a lot of time helping other newly arrived Chinese businesspeople deal with the maze of American tax laws. He even learned to speak a little Chinese.

That gave him an idea: Why not set up an accounting practice specializing in helping Chinese deal with the American tax system? He did just that. And it was more successful than he ever dreamed.

He even ran an ad in the local Chinese newspaper.

Today his business is booming, and his niche—of helping Chinese deal with our confusing tax laws—has grown even faster since he started advertising.

His ad simply says: "American accountant who speaks Chinese, and can help you understand our crazy tax system."

In the staid and stuffy world of accountants, he definitely has an outstanding USP. A USP that stands out and speaks to his audience in a friendly way.

5. If You Have a Slogan, Is It Memorable Enough to Continue for Years?

Pepsi has been promoting the "Pepsi Generation" for more than twenty years.

And Maxwell House coffee is still "good to the last drop."

A friend of ours has had a bed-and-breakfast in Vermont for twenty years. She has a sign out front that continues to encourage tourists to stop and choose her place over all others. She says: "I can hear the cars slow down; sometimes they slam on their breaks."

The sign simply states: DELICIOUS BEDS. DELICIOUS BREAKFASTS.

6. Can You Deliver on the Promise Your Brand Makes?

Repeat business—in any business—is the key to success.

Now that you have completed the checklist and have made sure that your name matches the unique brand you wish to create and helps reinforce your USP, check to make sure that your unique brand is in sync with your personal and professional mission and your business plan or road map. Your dream can come true if your plan has these three key elements, fitting together in one coherent whole.

The Courage to Make Big Promises— and the Will to Deliver on Them

Your dream of tomorrow must be perceived by your prospective customers as today's reality.

"Nobody on God's earth ever told me what it was going to be like. I couldn't believe what I had to promise to get the business."

—John Coe, owner and president of Rite Engineering

As a successful entrepreneur, you must learn to dream with your eyes open and find ways of making others see your *dreams* as today's *reality*.

This is very different from what you have learned in corporate life, where you can succeed by being extremely cautious in promising anything to anybody. In fact, often the most successful people in the corporation are those who are the best at defending the status quo rather than dreaming great dreams about the future.

Yet when you follow your dream and become an entrepreneur, you must be able to describe your vision with such power and confidence and courage that your dream takes on the form of an *irresistible reality.* We call the ability to clearly describe your dream with such force the capacity to make the *Big Promise.* To become a successful entrepreneur you have to have the courage to make the Big Promise and the will to deliver on it.

As an entrepreneur, you will frequently find yourself in the position of having to portray your business as being in the place you want it to be rather than the start-up it currently is, in order to convince a customer to give you the business in the first place. In other words, you need to present your first customer with the Big Promise as though it were today's reality.

A Big Promise: Promising International Resources to a Customer While Still More of a Dream Than a Reality

When Sheila was starting her company with one partner and one part-time employee, she had an opportunity to present to a major international food company. This was a customer that Sheila badly wanted, for she knew that they could be the first big organization that would give her the credibility and stature she needed to achieve her dream. If she could bring on such a customer, others would surely follow.

And she knew that they needed her and an organization like the one she dreamed of building. For the company had few marketing people in Eastern Europe and would probably leap at the chance to get some help in that area. *If* they believed she were "for real."

Yet—at the time she went to them—Sheila's business dream was far from a practical reality. For her dream envisioned several offices in Eastern Europe while she was then working with just her partner and one part-time employee out of one office in New York.

She knew that to get this business she would have to describe her dream of the future, rather than simply her current reality. And she knew she would have to describe her dream with such force and power that they would believe it would come true— that she could become a presence in Eastern Europe and that she would be able to deliver the resources to answer their large and growing needs.

She began her meeting by reminding them of the USP she had used over the phone to set up this key meeting: "Let us be your marketing arms and legs and brains in Eastern Europe—without the overhead." Her USP was, in this case, also her Big Promise— for in a sense Sheila was promising resources that she only dreamed of having. Yet her USP, her Big Promise, had gotten her this meeting.

They were impressed enough by her USP to be eager to listen to her.

During this major meeting, Sheila went on to describe what she would do for them. Sheila spoke as though she *already had* the offices and experienced staff she envisioned hiring, and *already had* the experience she knew would come.

At the end of the meeting she repeated her Big Promise. Sheila got the business. And then Sheila went to work to make sure she could *deliver* on the Big Promise. This can often be the most hair-raising time for any entrepreneur.

Sheila spent many sleepless nights figuring out how to deliver for her first major customer. But she *did* deliver. She built the organization and resources that they needed to succeed in their marketing objectives. Once she had the business from them, she was able to move forward confidently to hire the people and open the offices she needed to make her dream a reality.

She built her future business on the strength of that first success.

But Sheila would never have gotten a *chance* to build her business unless she had had the *courage* to make a Big Promise and the *will* to deliver on it.

Sheila's lesson, which we will dramatize with further examples, is that—no matter what size your business is—as an entrepreneur you have to have the courage to make a Big Promise to get your business going.

A Big Promise: Posing as a Major American Importer While Still a Junior Employee of an Accounting Firm

Phil Knight, founder and still chief executive of Nike Corporation, had a clear idea of what kind of business he wanted—from the very beginning. He wanted to build a big business selling running shoes. And he wanted to do it with the use of Japanese manufacturers.

Yet when he first went to Japan to talk to potential manufacturing partners, he was still a junior employee of a major accounting firm. Knight realized that his current position would not carry much weight with the status-conscious Japanese he was hoping to impress. So he described himself as he *dreamed* of being: as a successful American businessman who could give manufacturers of running shoes wide distribution in the American market. His *dream* of being a big and successful importer of running shoes manufactured in Japan became the *reality* he presented to his potential Japanese partners. That was Phil Knight's Big Promise.

It worked. He was able to sign contracts with a top Japanese manufacturer. They gave him their business based on the power of his vision—he convinced them that his *future dream had already come true.*

Phil Knight returned to America with the major contract he needed to start his business and make his dream a reality.

And then he *delivered on his Big Promise,* by building a great distribution system for his Japanese partners. His business grew so much, as his Big Promise became a profitable reality, that he was able to resign from his job at the accounting firm. He became the major American businessman, and seller of running shoes, he had always dreamed of being.

But it is wise to remember: Nike would never have gotten off the ground, Phil Knight would never have been able to become a billionaire, unless he had had the courage to make a Big Promise and the will to deliver on it. And the same will be true for you.

A Big Promise: Promising a Product You Have Yet to Create

Bill Gates is another entrepreneur who got his start in the business by his ability to make a Big Promise and then deliver on it.

Gates had always had a clear idea of what he wanted to be: the prime software supplier to the world. He thought he was the best in the world at designing software. But he needed a chance to start a business on that premise.

While he was still an undergraduate at Harvard, he heard that the then most popular maker of portable computers needed new software for their machines. He and his partner, Paul Allen, called

Altair, the computer manufacturer, at their headquarters in Albuquerque, New Mexico. Gates promised this huge potential customer that he could have a software package that was ideal for his computer.

That was his Big Promise.

He then dropped out of Harvard and proceeded to deliver on the Big Promise by actually creating the software.

He barely made it—but the software worked. Bill Gates and Paul Allen moved to Albuquerque, New Mexico, to be near their first and biggest customer. That was where they launched Microsoft.

Gates's Big Promise, and fast delivery, enabled him to get the greatest software company in the world off the ground.

Big Promises, when they are delivered on, can lead to big gains. But—at the very least—such confident promises are needed simply to *survive* as an entrepreneur.

It is not a question of whether or not you should make a Big Promise. You will *have* to make such promises if you want your business to succeed.

A Big Promise: Saving Your Business by Going Beyond the Standard Guarantee

You probably remember John Coe from our earlier chapters. He's the person who bought Rite Engineering, a company that made boilers, a product that John, as a twenty-year employee of Anaconda Copper, had no previous knowledge of.

"I hadn't expected the boiler business to be so competitive," John says, "but after the first year it was clear we were not going to survive unless I did something. I'd learned enough to know that our boilers were first-rate, as good as any of the competitors'. But the trouble was that our potential customers didn't *know* me. I was completely new to the whole business. They had no reason to trust me. As an entrepreneur, I discovered that all business decisions come down to an individual trusting another individual. A boiler is a big investment, and I had to give them a reason to bet on me.

"So I made a decision that I was going to stand behind the boilers we made—even beyond the standard guarantee or basic boiler warranty. I took the stand that we had an obligation to help our customers when something went wrong even if it wasn't covered specifically by our legal guarantee.

"This was a revolutionary step in the boiler business, for boilers can be broken because they are mistreated by people in a variety of ways. And I had no control over what happened to the boilers once they were installed. When something did go wrong, I would work with the customer to fix it—even if the warranty no longer covered the particular problem. If the customer had a problem—my attitude was that I was going to help them fix it.

"I personally stood behind our product beyond the standard guarantee. Gradually, more and more customers came to know and to trust me. Today, we have built a very successful business. But if I hadn't been willing to go beyond the legal warranty, I don't think we would have survived."

A Big Promise: Presenting Your Work in the Way You'd Like It to Be Seen

John Saladino is a world-famous designer who launched the successful business he has today by the bold stratagem of convincing the *New York Times* to publish pictures of his work as an example of great designs. He knew that if he could convince the *New York Times* that he was already an established interior designer, he could become one. (He was then a frustrated lowly employee at a big architectural firm.)

He succeeded in this amazing strategy by decorating his own apartment, at his own expense, paying a photographer to take pictures, then sending the photographs and the write-up to the *Times*, asking for publication in the Style Section.

At first he was turned down by the editor of the Style Section. She simply returned his photographs with a polite rejection note. But some months later John Saladino saw that she had left her position in a corporate shuffling. This is where John showed the courageous genius that made him a deservedly successful entrepreneur. He decided to invent a Big Promise for himself, and deliver it to the *Times.*

He immediately sent his package of his photographs and an enthusiastic write-up to the *new* editor of the Style Section, implying that the previous editor of the *Times* had asked him to have it done.

The new editor did not know he was pretending and promising to be something that he was not—yet! She accepted John Saladino as an established and known interior designer. When the pictures appeared in the *Times*' Sunday Magazine, in the favorable context that John had created, potential clients immediately started calling.

John then—and this is the important point—was able to deliver on his early pretense and Big Promise potential. He did some innovative interiors for his first clients, and they spread the word, and he did, indeed, become truly well known and famous as a great designer.

But it all started with his own creation: a Big Promise he created and then delivered, without the *Times* realizing they had never asked for such a promise in the first place.

It is continually surprising how successful entrepreneurs can be when they have the courage to make a Big Promise and the will to deliver on it.

Big Promises Are Tricky; They Can Break Your Business if You Can't Deliver When You Said You Would

In business, as in life, timing is everything. And if you make a Big Promise, you have to deliver on it when you said you would.

One entrepreneur told us of a problem he had when leading a biotech firm in northern California. The firm promised that a breakthrough product would be delivered within a year. When a year passed and the product was still not yet in the market, supporters and financial backers were disappointed. The firm lost credibility with its most important potential customers.

A Big Promise is needed to succeed, but not delivering on time can kill you faster than any other single factor. A Big Promise that you don't deliver on can haunt you more than any other business mistake.

Too Many Promises

One entrepreneur ran an architectural firm that almost went out of business the first year it started. The firm got so many commissions and ran in so many different directions, it disappointed a lot of clients. It lost its focus and ended up making too many promises to too many people.

You can destroy yourself by promising too much too soon. It is better, when just starting out, to focus on making one Big Promise and then delivering on it, rather than trying to promise many things to many people and then failing to keep all those promises.

You only have a certain amount of time and a certain amount of resources; don't scatter them.

Bill Backer ran into the same kind of problem. At the Backer & Spielvogel advertising agency, he and his partner would promise clients that they would personally be involved in their business. But, as the business grew, they became more and more stretched. They realized they would have to limit their business to a few key clients if they were going to keep their Big Promise of being personally involved in the clients' business. When they limited their promise to one that they could deliver, their business succeeded.

Choosing the Wrong Promise to Make to Your Customer

Another entrepreneur left a top job at a major consulting firm to run a food franchise business. He hadn't actually ever run a business before. And he tended to overreact to any problems.

When the business began to slow down, he decided that he would offer liquor to improve his profit margins.

This was not a good idea, for it took a great deal of time and effort to try to get liquor licenses in all the different states his stores were in. Even worse, it turned out that being able to offer drinks was not a key promise for his customers. His business didn't improve.

He should probably have concentrated on serving better food faster, instead of running after the difficult goal of introducing liquor into his restaurants.

Conclusions

Leave Your Corporate Caution Behind—Make a Big Promise to Get the Business!

A conservative, corporate style will not work for Life in the Wild. You have to make Big Promises and deliver on them to survive, let alone succeed.

If You Can Dream It, You Can Do It

The good news is that there is a lot of proof that by having the courage to make a Big Promise you are already a long way toward achieving it.

There is an awesome truth: Enthusiastically presented promises can take on an incredibly powerful *reality.* There is a wonderful way the world will take you at your word.

But if you wish others to believe in you, you have to believe in your dreams enough to treat them not as favorite fantasies, but as today's reality. You have to enthusiastically describe and confidently live your dream of the future—today! You have to make the Big Promise.

Then your vision of the future will be accepted by your potential customers as a reality they can also believe in and commit to by giving you their business.

When You Make a Big Promise, Be Willing to Do Whatever It Takes to Deliver on It

Entrepreneurs should not expect second chances. When you make a Big Promise, do everything possible to deliver on it.

By making a Big Promise and delivering on it, you will successfully launch your business. There is no other way.

Be Prepared to Be a Confident Star in the Show of the Self-Employed. The Show is Entitled: *Smiling Through!*

The Disney Company has a wonderful orientation program for new employees. It is called, naturally enough, Disney University. There, you learn that your sole mission is: to create happiness for Disney's customers.

The way you are taught to go about creating that happiness is by creating a conscious and consistent illusion that you are having a wonderful time every minute of every day. The maintenance of this illusion of happiness takes great discipline from everyone who is hired by Disney. The workers, cleaners of toilets, takers of tickets, mouseketeers, and marketers must never appear to be unhappy, upset, or worried about their lives—that would interfere with the illusion so essential to a visit to Disneyland.

Now, it is rather unnatural never to let an honestly unhappy look ever cross your brow. Yet Disney achieves this unnaturally upbeat expression in the faces of thousands of troops by telling them they are no longer to reflect on their own problems, but to think, instead, of themselves as onstage. They become cast members. Performers in one of the most successful, longest-running shows in the world of business.

As an entrepreneur, you are also part of a vital show. A show that, to be successful, must have you as a positive, upbeat, happy star.

You could term this entrepreneurial show the show of the self-employed: *Smiling Through!* For a smile will not only win you business, but keep the business you have won.

Once you have successfully made a Big Promise and are in the depths of panic in delivering on it, you must never let your positive, confident face slip—if you want your prospective clients to have confidence in you. Which they *must* for you to succeed.

Just as a great doctor has to have a positive bedside manner and an upbeat attitude as he wheels you in for your operation, you must present to your clients and your employees—even to your best friends—a confident belief that you will clearly fulfill the Big Promise you have made.

One story will illustrate the dangers of ever dropping this starring stage role for real life.

One entrepreneur was having lunch with a former corporate colleague. She happened to casually mention that she was having trouble getting money from some of her clients. Two weeks later she heard that one of her competitors was spreading the rumor that she had cash flow problems and might be going out of business. That's how fast bad news—right or wrong—can spread.

The slightest sign of any negative concern can sink your business.

If you have the urge to burst into tears—do it in the privacy of a tiny room in some mountain retreat somewhere. Alone. And then go back onstage and knock them dead with your positive performance. One entrepreneur told us, "The day I became a success was the day I realized that *everybody* was a prospective client—so I had to be at my best with everyone I met."

The world of successful entrepreneurs is full of smiling faces and confident attitudes. And there is reason for you to be happy. When you have the courage to make a Big Promise and the will to deliver on it, good things usually happen. And they will continue to happen as long as you keep playing your confident role in the show of the self-employed.

The Big Promise and the confident show of the self-employed are self-fulfilling prophesies. This is true among all the successful entrepreneurs we have studied.

And it will be for you.

Fired Up! Fired Up! Fired Up! Fired Up! Fired Up! Fired Up! Fired Up! Fired Up! Fired Up! Fired Up! Fired Up! Fired Up!

200

The Quick and
the Dead

"As a corporate employee I used to just *spend* my time in a lot of different ways that I look back on, now that I'm an entrepreneur, as time wasted. Now I've learned to *invest* my time in a focused way that really pays off for me and for my business."

—Cameron Estes, president of ELEK-TEK,
a successful entrepreneur in the retail business

When working for a corporation, you become accustomed to a very structured idea of time—a time that can be divided with mathematical precision into neat blocks. You learn to categorize your day: So much time spent for lunch, so much time spent for dinner. Even, two or three times a year, so much time spent for vacation.

As an entrepreneur, time takes on a new and more vital dimension.

Successful entrepreneurs don't segment their time into neat categories; every second of entrepreneurial time is seamlessly linked, focused and fused together by the overwhelming passion to achieve dreams. Thus, every second counts. Every moment of entrepreneurial time becomes a valuable *investment* in making your own dream come true.

This is not a chapter on time management. There are many excellent books on the subject, and we include some recommendations in the appendix. This chapter focuses on how you must take a *new view of your time,* and the intricate, indivisible, and important relationship between your time and your money and being able to build your business in a successful way.

Because each moment becomes so valuable and because each second is, indeed, an investment in your own business, entrepreneurs discover that . . .

There Is Never Enough Time

John Childs told us: "Before I left Prudential, where I had spent seventeen years, I was worried that I wouldn't have enough to do when I started my own business. I worried that my phone wouldn't ring. I shouldn't have worried."

It is just the opposite. You quickly discover that you simply don't have enough time. Why? Because in setting up a new business or in buying a business, there is so much you have to learn and do that you've never done before. And this truly takes an enormous amount of time.

One entrepreneur told us: "I was really afraid going out. I knew there were so many things I didn't know. In a corporation you could depend on people in accounting, marketing, or human resources—and demand their support. When you are out on your own, there is none of that.

"As an entrepreneur, you've got to quickly learn and perform effectively in areas that you're unfamiliar with. And this takes time—lots of time. You've probably heard about a typical entrepreneurial work day of eighteen hours six or seven days a week. . . . You probably heard about it, but didn't really believe it. *Believe it.* I love the freedom of being able to choose which eighteen hours during the day I want to work! Virtually every entrepreneur I know puts in this kind of time."

From the very first day in your new business, you will find yourself viewing time very differently.

Remember those relaxed phone conversations you had when friends called you at the office? As an entrepreneur you'll find yourself trying not to be rude when getting off the phone as fast as possible. No more coming in after a weekend and spending fifteen minutes talking about what you did with a close buddy in the office. You begin to realize that those fifteen minutes could have been used to help your business move forward. They could have been used to make money. Your relaxed days are over.

Every entrepreneur we have talked to feels that time takes on a whole new dimension of value when they are investing it in their own business and working so hard to achieve their own dream.

There is a saying: "You can never be too thin or too rich." For entrepreneurs, there is a saying: "There is never enough time!"

Networking Can Become Your Enemy

In corporate life, you are encouraged to network. It is important for your career to keep in contact with others in your business or in related areas. And there's always the added benefit of keeping up on what other job opportunities are around. However, when you are an entrepreneur, networking, unless properly controlled, can become your biggest enemy. It is often simply a waste of your time—or worse.

When Sheila went into her own business, within weeks of opening her office the networking started. A friend of a former business colleague heard that she was starting a business in the global consulting area and called to say that he wanted to talk with her.

Naturally, Sheila thought that meant a potential client had called. She prepared for the meeting to present their credentials. Imagine her surprise when instead of presenting credentials, she was presented *to,* and at the end of the meeting was asked whether or not she had any business for the networker. It even went a step further. The networker went on to ask if she could use an employee who was savvy about global marketing. In other words, the networker had called, after all that, in hopes of getting a job.

This is not an isolated incident. No matter what new business you start, the word will go out almost immediately, and you'll find that you are inundated with calls from people who want to talk to you about business. Entrepreneurial leaders attract others. The difficulty becomes in separating the legitimate calls from those that are not. You don't want to pass up the opportunity for business, but you also don't want to waste time with people who have nothing to offer your business.

Networking on planes is particularly dangerous. When you become more experienced, you will be able to recognize the signs of a time-wasting networker. Usually such networkers are much too enthusiastic about your business and much too eager to talk to you about it. You realize that instant enthusiasm usually connotes someone looking for a job rather than someone who might help give you business. People who are eager to take your card and can't wait to call you are usually going to ask you for something rather than offer you something.

As an experienced entrepreneur you will become adept at making quick decisions about whether someone you meet is a potential prospect or a possible networking nightmare. In fact, being able to make quick decisions about a whole host of issues becomes a necessity.

Business-Threatening Decisions Have to Be Made on an Hourly, Even Minute-by-Minute Basis; If You're Not Up to Making Quick Decisions and Living with Them—Don't Start Your Own Business

How often do you have to make major decisions affecting the entire business life of your corporation when you are simply another employee? Not very often. And usually employees tend to avoid such decisions when they do come up. Often the smartest move for a corporate employee is to avoid making too many major decisions, as these are usually very risky. There are many who rise up the corporate ladder by avoiding such risks.

And even for those who are willing to make such major decisions, building a corporate consensus behind them can take so much time that it is hard, if not impossible, to act on such decisions for months or years.

Life for an entrepreneur is very different. In a corporation you can afford to *spend* your time. As an entrepreneur, you must *invest* your time in building your business. And that investment will often consist of major decisions. Your time will be *filled* with major decisions: Where will your business be located? Will you have a partner or not? What is your plan for success? What is your USP?

In addition to those major strategic decisions will be hundreds, even thousands, of tactical decisions you will have to make—every minute of every day. Should you fly halfway around the world to meet with a major prospect—or spend your time instead preparing for tomorrow's meeting with a key customer? You have two customers calling about a problem; which call do you put on hold? One of your new employees wants to quit; do you give him a raise or let him go? All those decisions can often occur within a five-minute entrepreneurial time span.

Because time is so precious, it is important that you plan, as we have said in earlier chapters, to make your dream come true *before* you have to live it. But even with the best planning in the world, you will still find that every second is precious—for it can affect how successfully you build your business.

One of the biggest dangers in living entrepreneurial time is that in such a fast-paced atmosphere, it is easy to lose track of how you are really investing your time. Which could be fatal for your business—financially.

Some Timely Advice

No Matter What Your Business, You Must View Your Time as Money

You've heard the expression: "Time is money." No matter what business an entrepreneur is in—whether you become an accountant, a manufacturer, a consultant, or a retailer—you've got to view your time as money.

Earlier we touched briefly on the importance of putting a proper value on your time. But it is critical to emphasize the fact that how you value your time will either make you successful or put you out of business.

Consultants frequently view their time on a billable hour basis. In other words: How much of my time is being covered by a client paying me for a particular job? What we recommend is that, whatever your business, you start viewing your own entrepreneurial time in exactly the same way. Whether you own a retail store or a manufacturing operation, you must value your time in terms of how it is related to bringing in money.

Of course, managing and administrating your company will also be critical to the success of your company and must always be taken into consideration. But as your guiding rule we find that most successful entrepreneurs learn to view their daily hours with one basic criterion in mind: At the end of each day they ask themselves, "What did I do to actually make money today?" In this way you can separate productive time from time-wasting.

Your Time Is a Business Investment Just Like Money

You may not think you are investing a lot of money when you go into your business, if your business is selling knowledge—such as accounting or consulting—but you are. Remember, if you are investing your time, you are investing a lot more than you think.

There is also the opportunity cost associated with your time—the time that you are putting against one particular project that you could put against an even more profitable one. That is an opportunity cost just like investment analysts view opportunity costs. If you begin to view your time this way, then you will begin to put a realistic value on it.

One entrepreneur has built a successful business as a financial adviser to small firms facing major cash flow problems: "I help a company when they have their backs to the wall," he says.

But he also says that as his reputation has grown as a "financial doctor," more and more people feel free to ask his advice. "During my first five years in the business," he says, "I was inundated by requests from friends or friends of friends asking me to review their finances or look over the books of their company.

And because I was flattered by their respect and intrigued by their problems, I would try to help them—though this took quite a bit of time.

"But as my business got busier, it became more and more difficult to do. Also, I came to the stunning conclusion that the time I was spending on this exercise was costing me money! It took me a lot of time just to set up a meeting with such a 'friend.' When you included phone calls and meetings set up and canceled, it usually amounted to more than two hours! By the time we finally had a meeting and I had a chance to counsel with them, I would almost always feel compelled to send them a follow-up letter.

"Finally, I realized that I had to start charging for my time or I would continue to be losing a significant amount of time—and money!—on the whole operation. Now I charge a simple fee of two hundred fifty dollars per hour for a professional financial evaluation.

"Charging for time I used to give away has helped me greatly in two ways. First, I am now getting paid for my time, and second, by charging something I quickly separate the serious people from someone just looking for free financial advice."

What he discovered was that giving your time away can sink an entrepreneurial venture—and this is true for *all people* who work for themselves. If you give away your time, you are giving away your business.

One of the many pitfalls you have to watch out for is handling "favors" from former corporate friends. Corporate employees have little feeling for how important every moment is for the entrepreneur. Unknowingly, they can encourage you to spend, and therefore waste, time that you can never charge for. As an entrepreneur, you have to picture your time as though it were gold you were giving away—gold that your business could use to survive and grow another day.

To the *outside* world, including all those former corporate friends, you must present a picture of someone who is extremely disciplined about making sure you always place a high value on your time, and only invest it in the highest potential projects.

Inside, in your own operation, however, you might find yourself investing your time in doing whatever it takes to keep the business running.

If You Can't Do It Yourself, You Have to Pay for It

This next piece of timely advice might seem inconsistent with what we have just told you—that you have to view your time as a valuable item. You might question whether you should be using your time on such inevitable menial projects as changing fax paper, changing toner on the printer, or ordering supplies. Yet these jobs must be done, and should probably be done by you.

It's a trade-off that you've got to work out. How much money will these tasks cost you? If you are a very small business—and most start-ups are—then you simply cannot afford to bring in extra help to do such jobs.

The money you spend paying for these services could be put into something you have to pay for because you simply can't do it yourself—such as printing your stationery and business cards or installing your telephone.

Another way to multiply the value of your time is that, instead of having a secretary, you could bring in a business assistant (recent college graduates and MBAs looking for experience can be terrific in this role) who is willing to work for minimum pay and is a superior investment. But hiring such people means that you have to pitch in and be willing to do the menial tasks yourself. That's just one of the many reasons why—as an entrepreneur—you will find yourself working longer and harder than anybody else.

We feel that the menial tasks are worth doing because they save out-of-pocket *cash* that would otherwise simply be wasted.

There's No Time for Long-Term Investment Strategies; You Learn to Focus on Opportunities that Have the Biggest, Quickest Upside Potential

Here's a quick time-check you can use to gauge whether your time is being wisely invested at any particular entrepreneurial moment: If it's not profitable at the time you are doing it, you've got to stop what you are doing. Immediately!

Even with such a time-check, you will occasionally find yourself involved in an activity that can't possibly pay off—but keep those to a minimum. Remember, all it takes for you to fail is a one percent misunderstanding about what is really a profitable endeavor for you. A shift from *investing* your time to *spending* your time in the wrong endeavor can deflate your business like a slow, silent leak in a balloon.

You owe it to yourself, and your business, to develop a positive sense of the worth of every second of your time. And it is our experience that successful entrepreneurs quickly develop a finely tuned instinct for investing their time in high-profit opportunities.

Now that you have become focused on investing your time in the most profitable way, you also have to be equally demanding in the value of the time you receive from anyone you might hire.

Your time is too valuable to be compromised by working with people who can't match your commitment and are not willing to invest their every effort in every second—an enthusiastic attitude that is absolutely essential for entrepreneurial success.

There's No Time to Accept Mediocrity— It Can Cost You Dearly

An entrepreneur leading a manufacturing firm in the South says his business almost went under because he wasn't tough enough about requiring a high level of commitment from everyone in the organization. The prime example of that was his chief financial officer, whom he inherited from the previous president. The CFO had done a fine job in the corporate world and probably could have continued to do a fine job there. He just wasn't ready for the quick, demanding pace that an entrepreneurial firm requires to succeed. He was used to taking his time and not seeing every instant as a precious resource.

This entrepreneur found that his top financial person was consistently overoptimistic, and undercommitted. The CFO just wasn't willing to put in the late nights and weekends required to really understand the business and help it move forward.

"I should have given the guy a chance to leave right away," he says now. "As it was, it took me a year of trying to get him to rev up to the necessary speed. I would have been much better off if I'd made a quicker personnel decision. He cost us dearly both inside and outside our organization. And he slowed us down when we had to move forward even faster. Now we are left having to make up for lost time—always a position that is tough to handle. I would have been much better off and so would he if I'd acted quicker."

Quick personal decisions are essential for success in an entrepreneurial business. You simply can't afford to spend the time carrying an individual who isn't right for a job. A corporation might be able to afford to carry people on its payroll who devote a below-average amount of energy and are not always suited to or enthusiastic about their roles. As an entrepreneur, you need to make sure that everyone you hire is as fired up as you are.

You Must Take the Time to Be Involved in Every Decision That Affects You Economically; These Cannot Be Delegated

Finances are the lifeblood of every business, and as an entrepreneur you cannot delegate that responsibility to anyone else, or else you can lose your business.

An entrepreneur had left a big corporate job and bought a small company that manufactures reclining chairs. At the big corporation, he had taken many training sessions in how to delegate. Delegation was regarded as a great art. The higher you went at his corporation, the more you learned to delegate.

So, naturally, when he became head of his small entrepreneurial chair business he tried to delegate—just as he had been taught. Within the first week his shop steward came in and told him he could make a much better product if the steward was only given his own way. The shop steward told him that the previous owner had never given him a chance to do what he was capable of in managing the production line. The entrepreneur delegated that effort to the shop steward, saying: "Do what you have to do to make a great product."

A year later he had an excellent product, but at a cost that almost put him out of business. It was an expensive, almost financially fatal mistake. The shop steward had ordered fancy new machines and given virtually everyone in manufacturing a big raise. He had created an overhead that was impossible to make work and still sell the product at a competitive price.

At the same time he was delegating financial decisions to his shop steward, the entrepreneur was delegating health plan decisions to his director of personnel. She told him that she was unhappy with their old health plan, that it was second-rate. He told her: "Do what you feel is best." The personnel director designed a great health plan for the company—but it took him a year to realize that it would bankrupt the company to continue with it.

Financial decisions about health plans or capital investments or raises are all properly the purview of the entrepreneur. *There are no small financial decisions.* Our entrepreneur spent a year of delegating, and it almost cost him his business. He had to give an infusion of his own money to pay the staff and to keep the business going. He had to do this for three years.

"I only had three Sundays off in three years," he says, "and I'm not a workaholic, but if I hadn't put the time in I would never have been able to figure out how to turn it around. I realized I couldn't delegate anymore, I had to get in there, roll up my sleeves, learn the business, and make sure I was involved in every decision about every dime that was spent."

His biggest lesson: "Don't delegate a penny."

Don't Waste Time Agonizing About What You Should Have Done—It Can Put You Out of Business

Don't waste time thinking about what you should have done—mistakes will happen. Successful entrepreneurs learn from their mistakes—quickly—and then move forward aggressively.

Everybody makes mistakes. A successful entrepreneur says: "I wear my mistakes like a badge of honor. "Anytime I have a major problem I make sure it won't happen again. I can't protect myself against the unknown, but I can about the known.

"You can't lose your confidence about making decisions. Making your own decisions is what being an entrepreneur is all about. And being able to make decisions is also a large part of the fun and satisfaction in being your own boss. No matter what it takes, you must make a decision, and if you make a mistake—which you are bound to do occasionally—instead of brooding over the mistake, which can be distracting and pull on the time you need to move your business forward, use it as a lesson. Every mistake is a lesson learned."

He has a good way of analyzing a mistake so that he can get the most out of it. He calls it "maximizing the mistake."

"I look on every mistake as an opportunity to do something better. A mistake is a problem waiting to be solved. I compare such problem-solving to a square. You have to solve the problem so all four sides of the square are closed. If you just fix the bottom of the square, there are still three sides that are left open. Even when you have the problem boxed in on three sides, it can still escape. You must try to think of boxing the problem in, and you can't just deal with one or two sides.

"Most entrepreneurial problems have at least four sides. This problem-solving technique forces you to look at them. Often problems have a personal side, a customer side, a financial side, and a quality side. The box is just a way of making the mistake into something you can analyze. Figure out why you made the mistake, then you can maximize the mistake as a learning process. And that makes the best use of your time. Otherwise, you might make the same mistake again. And that is a big, sometimes fatal *waste* of time."

Technology Is a Time-Saver and Essential to Your Business Growth—But Be Careful About Getting Too Involved in Your Computer Toys, for It Can Cost You Time and Money

Technology can be great multiplier of your time and efforts, or an expensive time-waster. Here are tips about how to keep technology as a tool to help you get where you want to go at an accelerated pace—rather than as an end in itself.

- Learn what you can while you are still employed at a big corporation. Your corporation will probably be happy to help you improve your technological IQ. Take every course you can—on their time. When you are out on your own, you won't have the time.
- Computer literacy is becoming the universal language of business. You have to be an early adapter. And you can't afford to waste precious time because you are computer-illiterate. So get the basics. Your business will drive you to acquire and learn the rest.
- Don't invest too much money in the very fanciest technology. Both your business and the technology you might need are advancing so quickly, it is not wise to invest too much at any particular time. Flexibility is key, keeping your options open. Throughout the last two decades, technology has gotten cheaper and better, and at an impressive rate.
- A final tip that we've mentioned before but needs to be reemphasized is the danger of becoming a technoholic. Be careful of getting caught in the trap of total involvement with your computer. Believe it or not, we know people who became so enamored of what their computer can do that they lost sight of why they bought the computer in the first place. A computer

is a tool to make your time more valuable, to multiply the speed at which you can work. Being lost in the Internet can be a big time-waster. Beware of such distractions. *Remember: The difference between the quick and the dead is the value and focus they put on using their time to the best advantage.* Entrepreneurial time is too valuable to spend on frivolous games or, even worse, in killing time on the Internet. Every second of entrepreneurial time should be seen as your most important *investment in achieving your dream.* Now the best use of your time is to turn the page and take a test designed to give you an excellent feeling of whether or not you are truly ready for the life of the entrepreneur.

The Ultimate Test

ARE YOU UP TO THE CHALLENGE OF BEING AN ENTREPRENEUR? THIS IS YOUR LOW-RISK, HIGH-REWARD CHANCE TO ANSWER A SERIES OF KEY QUESTIONS AND TAKE YOUR DREAM FOR A TEST-DRIVE.

1. Am I a worrier?

If you're worried about answering this question, that's a good sign. Worriers are winners in the world of the self-employed.

This is a quality that cannot be learned . . . only dramatically expanded. Ask a friend: "Am I a natural worrier . . . continually restless with the status quo?" If your friend says yes, go for it.

2. Am I the fastest person I know?

Quick, answer the question. If you are starting your own business, you've got to get back to people faster with better answers than anyone else.

Time's up. What's your answer?

3. Am I willing to look before I leap?

Before rushing rapidly ahead, it is essential that you decide on your destination and the way you intend to get there. In other words, before you leap, you have to look. You have to *write* down *what* you want to do and *how* you will do it. Creating a one- or two-sentence mission statement and a one- or two-page road map is a way to ensure that you can achieve your dreams. Then you have to pause a moment longer to make sure you can come up with a unique selling proposition (USP) in ten words or less.

And *then* you can begin to work to make your dream come true. And you will work like you've never worked before.

4. Am I willing to give up paid vacations . . . any vacations?

We have not met a successful self-employed person who goes on vacation. Maybe there is one—somewhere. A long weekend is the most you will get. Of course, you will also be able to squeeze in special trips when you decide it is worthwhile.

But if *you* are the business, you just can't shut down—even for birthdays or special occasions.

5. Am I my own best fan? Can I build my own brand?

The best entrepreneurs have an almost psychotic belief in themselves. Like great artists, they see the world differently. They believe that their ideas, their needs should take center stage. They are able to take this infantile perspective and somehow manipulate the world around them to accept it—at least long enough to give them a chance. If they succeed, they are a genius; if they fail, a fool.

Do you believe in your unique difference enough to promote yourself into a major brand personality?

If you had it to do over again, would you still fall in love with yourself?

Do you have this crazy belief in yourself and your ideas? Let's be completely frank: Are you a little bit crazy?

Great entrepreneurs are "crazy" until they make it, and prove the world wrong and themselves right. Can you really be your own best fan, and build your own unique brand, during that challenging time . . . when the whole world doubts you?

6. Can I handle the loneliness *and* the togetherness?

This is the loneliness of the long-distance runner. Leave all your old team analogies behind. Leave all your old friends behind. You can't even share your problems with your former best friends. For if you confide your troubles, they will pass it on. And you want word to spread about your success—not your anxiety.

So you must absorb all your anxieties yourself. Can you take that lack of human, team-sport activity? Are you that much of a loner?

On the other hand, as an entrepreneur you may find that you have to work with a partner. Do you know how to pick a partner? For many entrepreneurs, picking the right partner is one of the most fateful decisions.

7. Do I love my home?

In the brave new world of the self-employed, homes should not be confused with offices. If you try to work at home, without establishing clear emotional as well as physical separation, you'll make your home a hell.

Your office becomes your natural home, your overnight bag, a bureau. Can you take the peripatetic lifestyle that many entrepreneurs find so essential? Is your portable computer your favorite traveling companion? If you answered yes to both questions, we've saved the toughest one for now . . .

8. Am I addicted to my paycheck?

Paycheck dependency is sometimes an incurable disease.

As you think about the answer to this question, consider whether you really want to shop for your own medical insurance and watch your own taxes—every last dollar of them.

Without a paycheck, you discover the importance of cash flow, and your accountant has to become your best friend. Do you really want to give up the relative ease of having a whole accounting department at your beck and call?

A steady paycheck also impresses serious people when you

want to buy a house or own a car—or even make a trip. Lack of a paycheck does not instill confidence in anybody.

Is your freedom from the corporate world so vital to you that it is worth dealing with all the details formerly handled by your employer? Including the detail about getting paid, on time and with checks that never bounce? Hassling people for money is one of the least fun and most necessary entrepreneurial activities.

This question about being paid every two weeks rather than gambling every hour of your future is an important one. Perhaps the most important one. That's why we put this question in. If you are not sure of your answer, you don't have to complete the test.

On the other hand, no one can really count on a corporate paycheck in the nineties. For tomorrow the paycheck might turn to a pink slip. Which is why we prepared this book for you.

And if you are still with us, despite all our warnings, you have already shown the determination that is—above all—the most important quality of the successful entrepreneur. So carry on!

9. Would I be willing to sacrifice family and friends for monetary gain?

The mark of every successful entrepreneur is his or her willingness to borrow from family and friends. You not only have to invest in yourself, you are going to have to ask others to do so.

You have to believe in your idea enough to make this request. Are you good at asking for money? A self-employed person with an idea has to be very good at marshaling financial resources.

Could you live with yourself if you borrowed from family and friends, and then went bust? Once again, this is part of the normal process for most entrepreneurs. Trying an idea and having it succeed at once is very rare.

10. Do I have the courage to make big promises—and deliver on them?

One of the toughest parts of making a go of it is that you have to make big, even incredible promises to prospects—or you won't succeed.

You have to say what *will* be as though it *is*—right at the moment—true. You have to promise a future as though it *already* existed. You have to promise what you hope will be—and then, somehow, some way, deliver. Can you promise a dream with great conviction and energy? Can you present so well that you and your customer believe the promise will come true at the moment of telling?

There is a powerful, convincing magic to this form of presenting—it enters the realm of art. It is like theater in which you persuade people, through the power of a credible vision, to enter a world that actually doesn't yet exist.

Are you the kind of person who can positively enjoy the experience of persuading others to believe something you know to be not quite true . . . quite yet? And then, even more important, are you the kind of person who can scramble to make your big promises *come* true? Then maybe, just maybe, you've got a chance . . . if you skate fast enough. Which leads us to our last question.

11. Do I enjoy skating on thin ice?

Ask yourself whether you really like the idea that you have no support.

At a large corporation, the ice is thick, made up of many layers of specialists who are there to support you. In fact, it is almost impossible to break through to the cold water beneath. You really have to work at it and dig a hole to get there.

But the ice of support for the self-employed is very thin. You can hear it cracking beneath you as you try to skate forward. Do you really want to chance falling in? The odds are good as an entrepreneur that every so often you'll take a cold bath, and be lucky to get out with your life. Henry Ford had several major business catastrophes before he found success. At thirty-eight, he was regarded by many as a failure. He'd fallen through the ice several times.

Could you stand that kind of public humiliation? People will gather around and sympathize, yet smile. For it is kind of a funny sight—someone skating on thin ice and then falling through.

But that is the essential situation of the entrepreneur. Does that prospect of having to skate so fast and live so dangerously excite you?

If you answer: "But isn't thin ice the natural condition of the nineties?" And if you would rather skate ahead, making your own trail, then the entrepreneurial world is the world for you.

It is a *real* world, the world outside the corporate zoo— a roller coaster of emotion, excitement, and adventure. Above all, it will be a world of your own, with success of your own making, rather than a secondhand life handed down through some corporate guidelines.

If you are ready to live life as we have honestly described it . . . you have passed the test.

Hang on tight. You are in for the greatest ride of your life.

The Ride of
Your Life

"**E**ntrepreneurs are like athletes: They really have to focus. Focus means that it's your life and you're thinking about it all the time. When you focus, the ideas flow, there's an excitement about it, and you know you're doing a great job and it's like being on cloud nine!"

> —*Marg VeneKlasen, a former high school coach and now president of VeneKlasen Property Management Company, one of the most successful property management companies in Santa Fe, New Mexico*

You could call this all-consuming focus the E-Zone—the Entrepreneurial Zone. The zone that successful entrepreneurs get into. A zone where everything comes together to help you and your business succeed.

To get in the E-Zone you have to work at it. You have to go through many of the steps described in this book. You have to learn to trust your "intelligent emotions." Use your fear to fuel your forward motion. Find a way to have an office—without making your home a hell. Discover whether or not you want to work with a partner; and find an accountant, a banker, and a lawyer you can use to make your business happen in the most effective and productive way.

You can't get in the E-Zone until you have clearly worked out your own personal and professional mission statement and have developed a road map to keep you on track, plus a USP that you are confident will give you the recognition you need to succeed.

You are in the E-Zone when you have the courage to make a Big Promise, and have the will to find a way to deliver on it. When you don't have to bother to cut your time into little chunks—but your days flow with a positive focus. When all these qualities become second nature, when there is a seamless certainty to your time, your business, and your life—you have entered the E-Zone.

Getting in the E-Zone Means Doing What Is Right for You

Once you are in the E-Zone, there is a clear, calm feeling that you have finally taken charge of your destiny. That you are now doing what you love to do, with the people you want, in the location you've chosen.

Sometimes entering the E-Zone can occur at an early age. For others, it can take a large portion of their working lives to muster the courage to let themselves go—to become the success they are capable of being.

When you do truly let yourself go, you will discover that in the E-Zone there are no limits. In the E-Zone you will be able to reap all the rewards your talents can bring you. You will have an energizing experience just like the entrepreneurial friends of ours quoted in this book who have gone out and achieved *their* dreams. Their own words are the best way to convey the enthusiasm and excitement they still feel.

"**I**t's the most empowering and fulfilling thing—and there isn't anything wrong with making a buck either!"

—*Marg VeneKlasen*

Marg says: "If you think raising five kids and having a successful marriage and starting a statewide soccer league for boys and girls is an exciting effort—that is nothing to what I've experienced since I set up my own business."

Marg says that life as an entrepreneur is the most demanding existence possible—but she loves it. "I never really get tired," she says, "because having your own business is so rewarding—it feeds you and it gets stronger and stronger!"

Marg set up VeneKlasen Property Management Company eight years ago and now it is a leader in the Santa Fe real estate market. "If women only knew what they could do," she says, "this world would be upside down!"

"**I** could have worked for a thousand lifetimes for Prudential and still not gotten the money I achieved in just a few years out on my own."

—*John Childs, former salaried employee—now one of the most successful investors in the world*

"When I worked at Prudential," John says, "there was a definite limit put on how much I could earn. Despite the fact that I was one of the senior executives, managing billions of dollars, I still could only be paid what was a limited, acceptable salary within a very conservative corporation.

"One of my primary jobs was investing Prudential's money in young entrepreneurial companies. I realized I was making a lot of entrepreneurs rich. I decided to become one myself."

"It's like raising a child—a business needs constant attention."

—*Marilyn Burns, former teacher, now founder and CEO of Marilyn Burns Education Associates, a multimillion-dollar teaching operation recognized by* Business Week *as one of the most successful entrepreneurial ventures of 1994*

"My business is as demanding as a growing child," Marilyn Burns says, "but I really get a great sense of satisfaction from building and running a company that can bring a positive dimension to the teaching experience. With my own company, I can expand my ideas many times across many classrooms.

"There is a revolution going on in the business world. I help people ride the wave of the future."

—*Kent Black, who has created a company, Kent Black & Associates, to help people achieve their dreams*

Kent Black, an entrepreneur who used to work for one of the leading outplacement firms and now has started his own business, says: "At first everyone thought that outplacement was just a fad that would go away. But it is not a fad, because companies have dramatically changed. There is always going to be downsizing. Even good, hardworking people are going to find themselves at a loss in a big company. They need help to find the life that is right for them."

Kent loves his work. "I love to work with people, and figure out what they should do. There is a moment of revelation when they realize they don't have to play by the old rules of corporate life. They can make their own rules. In America today, in the world today, there are so many opportunities it is really a question of choosing what you want to do, rather than worrying about whether or not you will be allowed to do it. I enable people to become entrepreneurs—whatever they decide to do—in the sense that I strongly encourage them to create their own business destiny."

Kent is one who helps people make the transition from the traditional workplace of yesterday to the satisfying, exciting entrepreneurial world of today.

"I had a wonderful fantasy—which I was able to live!"

—Gary Boyle, former advertising executive who had a dream to live in the Caribbean

"I had a typical fantasy," Gary Boyle says. "Like most people who have had a chance to vacation in the Caribbean, I came back to my corporate job determined to get out and find a way to live there.

"I bought a shopping mall, and built a successful real estate business that allows me to live not only in the Caribbean, but anywhere in the world I could want to be.

"Now I live the life I had only dreamed about!"

"**I** left a big job in a bank to build a business—and I would never go back!"

> —*John Gray, former vice president of a bank, now owner and marketer of Bubbies Pickles of San Francisco*

"I had always wanted to have my own business, yet I had never really known what a powerful experience it would be. It takes over your whole life. But the greatest feeling is that you are in charge—you don't have to defer your decisions to some committee. It isn't easy, but I would never go back to sitting in a bank!"

"**I**t's like being on the top of a mountain and watching all the people stuck in the traffic below."

> —*John Saladino, who moved from a junior position at a large architectural firm to one of the world's greatest and most distinguished designers*

John Saladino describes the entrepreneurial experience this way: "Having my own firm gives me the chance to go where I want to go, do what I want to do. You can see and do things you never thought possible.

"I am able to create with the artistic freedom I need. And I don't have to have a lot of people looking over my shoulder."

"**E**ach day is a creative act."

—Martin Braid, who worked with AT&T and is the recent creator of his own successful software company SQL Works Inc.

Martin says: "Each day I get to choose what I will do and who I will work for, and on what problems.

"I choose challenges that excite me. Nothing could be more creative."

"**I** couldn't design a better life. Come to think of it, I did design this life—maybe that's why I enjoy it so much."

—Caryn Mandabach, successful Hollywood producer

"I love working with some of the most creative people in the business world.

"I love taking time for yoga—which I do for an hour every day.

"I love being involved as a trustee with the kids' school, and spending time as a whole family with my husband.

"It's a life I've worked hard to create, and I'm very happy with it!"

"**O**n your own you're able to take risks and grow—the sky's the limit!"

—Matthew, Mark, and Luke Burke, brothers and partners in Kingsland Company, which has become one of America's leading church restoration operations

"It's the only way to get ahead," the brothers say. "We are always looking for a better way to help churches restore the beautiful woodwork they have. And we keep investing in our business to keep on top.

"We've been going for over a decade, and we have never had more work to do and our work has never been better."

"This one's for me!"

—*Judith Ets-Hokin, founder of HOMECHEF Cooking School and Kitchen Store*

Judith Ets-Hokin told us: "When I decided to get a divorce, I realized: Time is running out! I better live the life I wanted to—right away. I could see that I had spent too much time worrying about what others thought, and not enough simply going ahead with my own ideas. So I promised myself I would have my own business—and base it on cooking, which I love. And I did it. Getting out and starting my own business has been the greatest experience of my life!"

"Being an entrepreneur is the most liberating and invigorating thing you can do because it is constantly challenging and constantly making you grow and think!"

—*Cameron Estes, president and CEO of ELEK-TEK, a multimillion-dollar Chicago-based electronics operation now listed on NASDAQ, and former secretary to Sheila*

Cameron Estes says: "Building a business is a wonderful thing because it uses all your talents and energies. Nothing you have ever thought or felt goes to waste. Every day you are tested to be as good as you can possibly be.

"And the satisfaction when you can make it work—is enormous!"

"**I** am passionate about my business in a way I never thought possible!"

> —*Ludmilla Ivanovic, former waitress, now founder and owner of Iggy's, the best bakery in Boston*

"I have never felt such passion. It is like making love—only it goes on and on!" Ludmilla says.

"**I** think the best experience in business life is when you have your own business."

> —*Lambros J. Lambros, who went from company lawyer at major corporations to building Norfolk Holding, Inc., one of the most successful oil companies of its kind*

Lambros says: "My father came over from Greece. He arrived in Pittsburgh. Penniless. He went to work in the steel mills. He taught himself English. He saved his money. It was the Depression, and he saw everyone still found money to go to movies. So he bought a movie theater. And then a few more. He became a successful entrepreneur—even though he could hardly speak the language.

"I went to Harvard and Harvard Law School. Then I spent many years at the top of corporate America. It was interesting and certainly challenging in its own way. But being outside—building a business of my own—was the most fun I ever had."

"**A**s an entrepreneur, you get to make all the most important decisions—what you will do, who you will work with, where you will work. I love making such decisions!"

—Tom Margittai, former owner and operator of The Four Seasons restaurant

As an entrepreneur, you have to make a lot of decisions. Tom Margittai believes that one of the great satisfactions of being an entrepreneur is having control of your business. "You *are* the business," as Tom says.

"**T**he difference between being an employee and an entrepreneur is the difference between sitting in the backseat as a passenger or having a chance to drive your own car."

—David Davis, owner of the Pub Restaurant

"It hasn't been easy," David says, "but it is very satisfying. I have created a restaurant that I myself would like to visit. The Pub is successful in purely financial terms, but if you ask me what I really enjoy about the business I would have to say it was when I hear from people in the community who tell me how much they appreciate what I am doing. That's a great feeling!"

"**T**he best thing about my new life is having a chance to walk my daughter Bailey to school."

> —*Bill Woodhull, formerly a top government bond market professional for leading financial institutions, now an entrepreneurial owner of Beadworks stores*

"Officially," Bill says, "I'm the treasurer of Beadworks. My wife Eve is the president. But the title should be treasurer/handyman. I help out in every way I can." Beadworks is a company selling beads out of two busy stores.

"When you leave the corporate world it is a surprise how much you have to do—yourself," Bill says. "If there are boxes to move—I move them. But what I like best about my new life is the *flexibility* it gives me. My time is my own. That means I *can* take some time during the day to be with my wife and play with my daughter. If you asked Bailey, she might tell you I am one of her favorite playmates. And that is something I really like. I would have missed some wonderful times if I'd stayed on Wall Street."

"**C**reating an environment that is a meritocracy, where you're limited only by your own ability to get things done, is the joy of having your own business."

> —*Kate Newlin, creator of The Newlin Company, a successful New York public relations firm*

"**W**hen you become an entrepreneur you will have bought a ticket on the most exciting ride in the business world!"

*—Larry Goodwin, founder of Goodwin Manufacturing,
a successful manufacturing firm*

Larry says: "It is an emotional roller coaster, but it has also got to be by far the most exciting ride in the business world!"

The ride of the entrepreneur is, indeed, the best adventure the world has to offer. You will have a rewarding, exciting life that you will have the freedom to shape each day. For those of us who love it, this is life as it was *meant* to be.

A bumper sticker we saw in our travels says it all:

I LOVE MY BOSS. I LOVE MY JOB. I'M SELF-EMPLOYED!

We welcome you all to the E-Zone, and the great entrepreneurial world of today. Enjoy it! Be confident. *For you now know the dramatic truth of what it really takes to make the move from a fearful employee to a successful* Fired-Up! *entrepreneur.*

Appendix: Eleven Steps You Can Take Right Now Before You Leave Your Job

1. Ask Yourself Whether You Are Really Ready to Leave

Here are some questions to ask yourself:

- Do you get a sick feeling in the pit of your stomach on Sunday night at the prospect of going to work on Monday?
- Are you losing your temper at work more frequently?
- Do you feel as if you've gone as far as you can go in the company?
- Do you feel like your job is just one big repetition and contains no challenges?
- Have you spent more time planning a vacation than you ever have before?
- Are you getting sick more often and do you feel the need to take more sick days even when you have no physical illness?

- Are you finding yourself in meetings desperately trying to hold back a scream of frustration?
- Do you find yourself suppressing your instincts and your gut feelings in favor of doing what the boss wants?
- Do you hate your job at least sixty percent of the time?
- Is the prospect of getting a new boss really driving you crazy?

If you answered yes to at least seven of these questions, you're ready to leave. Read on. If you didn't, then you're probably not ready to leave your company. Our advice is that you dedicate yourself to doing an even better job where you are and rethink your career path.

2. Wake Up to All the Entrepreneurial Opportunities Around You

Begin to think of yourself not as a employee but as a successful entrepreneur. There have never been more opportunities for interesting entrepreneurial businesses than today. Four percent of the population—one in every twenty-five adult Americans—say that they're currently in the process of starting a company, according to a recent research survey by Paul Reynolds, chair holder of entrepreneurial studies at Marquette University. Think about how you can become one of these more than seven million incipient entrepreneurs.

With all these opportunities around you, you've got to decide what you really want to do. What do you really *love* to do? What are you really good at? The place to start is to determine how you can apply your proven expertise in the field in which you have been working and leverage it into your entrepreneurial business. In making this personal assessment, you've got to trust your "intelligent emotions"—if it feels right all the way into the pit of your stomach, it's probably right for you. List what you love to do and compare it to the experience you have. Is there a match? If not, there may be problems. We have found that for most entrepreneurs it is a lot easier and a lot less risky to launch a business from a base of some experience than going out cold.

It's also critical to share your thoughts and your plan with your spouse, children, or parents who are dependent on you as you go through these steps. People closest to you might have some valuable input in terms of what you might be good at. And you want to make sure that any decision you make doesn't come as a complete shock that they might react to in a negative way. You can't afford to have your private life come apart as you launch a new professional effort.

3. Determine What You Are Going to Do and How You Are Going to Do It

This step requires you to write down your specific business idea—what we've called your mission statement—in one or two sentences. We cannot stress enough the importance of writing down the basic business idea. Is this really a business that can make money or is it an unrealistic fantasy? Put yourself in the place of your prospective customer and ask yourself: Is what I'm offering a good idea? Is it better than other competitive products or services? If I were my customer, would I buy this? Research, research, research your business idea.

When Marilyn Burns decided to go into the business of helping schools improve how they teach mathematics, she tried each and every idea out in elementary classrooms until she was convinced that they improved students' learning, and then she translated those ideas into her training efforts and books for teaching. When she was convinced that she had good products, she knew her customers would be. When Martin Braid set up his business as a software designer, he leveraged his previous computer experience working for major corporations. He knew he had the determination and drive to create the very best software products, and he established his business with that mission. He used his experience to discover a need that was not being met by any other product on the market, and he invented a comprehensive add-on product to assist in the tuning of large relational databases—a niche market in a highly specialized field.

When you are convinced that your business idea is sound, then prepare your business plan, including the mission for the business and the road map to get you there. This can be as short as two or three pages, but like the original business idea, you must write it down. The very process of writing will clarify good ideas and point out the problems with bad ones. If you can't put it in writing, you've got to go back to step 2 and start over.

The business plan also must include revenue forecasts, how much you need to invest, how soon can you project that you will be able to start making money and taking a salary, and your cash flow requirements. Remember, no matter how good your projections are, without adequate cash flow and eventual profit, you'll go out of business. There are many books on the subject of business planning. Go to the library and find the one that seems closest to your type of business. Most of these books are not easy to read, but it is worth the effort. When you're finished with developing your business plan, don't think about it for two weeks and then come back to it and see if it still makes sense.

4. Plan to Stand Out in the Crowd

What is going to be the unique selling proposition (USP) that will successfully launch your business? Write it down. Does it stand out? SWOT your business by comparing it with three competitors. Does it offer a unique benefit to potential customers? Does it make your business sound better than the competition? Is this benefit better than what competitors can or do already offer? It is critical that you go through this process and carefully analyze what your existing and potential competitors are offering to give you what marketers call your "competitive advantage." A USP is not a USP unless it has this built-in competitive proposition. (For more about how to develop your USP we recommend *Reality in Advertising* by Rosser Reeves, published by Alfred A. Knopf, 1961, and distributed by Random House, New York.)

When Martin Braid created his new software product, he named it Index Master to reflect its superior index optimization techniques. This is its USP. When Marilyn Burns created her company, she called it Marilyn Burns Education Associates to instantly communicate the service she is delivering.

Can you describe *your* product or service in one memorable sentence? That's the test because that's about all the time you'll have. Using your USP, start practicing describing your business to a couple of your closest friends to see what they have to say. Ask them to be hard on you and to pretend that they are a potential customer. Then try it out on strangers on a plane or train or at a party, delivering the ideas as if it's a going business.

5. Decide Whom You Want to Work With

As you scout around for possible people who might be a partner, accountant, or lawyer with you, describe your business idea to them. Try out your USP on them. Listen to their responses to see if your skills can be complementary and their values are similar to yours. If they're not, keep looking.

Meet with your accountant and have him check the business numbers you have forecast. Does he understand your new business? Just because you have a terrific personal accountant doesn't mean he'll be right as your business accountant. Ideally you want to have an accountant who has experience with your kind of business. At the very least, your accountant should be very experienced with small business operations. A big corporate accountant will not know the guerrilla tactics required to make a small business work. Finally, for your own protection, choose an accountant who forces you to justify your revenue and cost forecasts. Your tendency will always be to be more optimistic in your forecasts. You need a tough, pessimistic accountant to offset your optimism, which is often unrealistic.

Once you've got your accountant's blessing, talk to your banker about your business idea in general terms. For example, ask about any predictions about the business environment in the field you are considering. (Be wary of exposing your plan to your banker too early in the process, as it might blow the possibility for future borrowing.) If you don't have a banker, ask other entrepreneurs which bank in your area seems the most supportive of new ventures.

Bring a potential partner into the process. Start with the breakfast meeting. What is he adding to the plan? How is he viewing his role relative to your role in the company? What is his vision for the company? Does it match your vision in terms of where you want to be in five years? How much money does he want to take out of the company—in the first year, in the second year? Be harder rather than softer in your measurement for each of these potential partners because right now you don't have to compromise, and compromise can be dangerous.

6. Pick a Place You Want to Live

This is not just the location of your office but where you want to spend your life. Is where you want to live consistent with the kind of business you want to do? Your business plan will offer critical input to help you determine where you can work. Martin decided he wanted to live in the country. In designing a software product, he could live anywhere. But that isn't true for all businesses, despite the technological revolution. For example, a young scriptwriter we know was forced to move from Chicago to Hollywood—because not too many people are producing TV shows in Chicago and he had to be where the TV action is. List your three most favorite places you want to live and then compare to number three in this list.

7. Choose a Date to Do It

Give yourself some specific deadlines and write down your time plan for launching your business. Figure out a win-win way to leave your present corporation. You want to leave so that you get as much money as you can and as much goodwill as you can before you go. Note: Don't walk into your boss's office and tell him you're going to leave. In fact, don't confide in anybody at work of your plans. Word could get out and this could force you to leave prematurely. Make sure your time plan includes all of the six previous steps in this list.

8. Play the Part

This is the opportunity to see if you will like doing the daily work involved in your new business as much as you thought you would. This is particularly critical if you're making a complete career switch. There is a big difference between a dream and the reality. If at all possible, use a vacation or find some opportunity to try out your business idea. Perhaps you can work for a week or two for free with somebody who has a similar business (but will not be threatened by you as a competitor). Visiting a restaurant, antique store, photography studio or a bed-and-breakfast is a lot different than working in one. Research the field; talk to people in the field; try to imagine yourself doing this work every day. The more you research, the better your chance for happiness and success.

9. Take the Moment-of-Truth Test

Make sure you can get at least one potential customer to sign up for your product or service *before* you launch your new life. Research confirms most people starting out do not devote full-time efforts to their new business until it's a going concern with one or more customers.

For example, an airline pilot we know recently opened a gourmet deli, and is running it in his spare time, while still employed.

Another example of trying out your idea before you go is when Mike told one of his clients of his plan to leave his firm and set up his own business. The client promised to hire him as a marketing consultant and in fact became his first customer.

It is important to note that this was a specific assignment that in no way hurt his old firm. It is advisable to always maintain a good relationship with your old company, because they frequently can help or hurt your new business efforts. One of the key referrals that Sheila first got was from the chairman of her previous company, who recommended her consulting firm to a major Fortune 500 client.)

If you can't get one person to buy your business idea before you leave, chances are you either don't have a good idea or you're not a good salesperson and you need to go back to square one or possibly look for a partner who can help you sell. This assessment may appear to be harsh; however, if you can't get the business while you've got the comfort of a paycheck, the odds are poor that you'll be able to get it when you're in the emotional turmoil of your new start-up. Many would-be entrepreneurs get so infatuated with their business idea or product that they forget that the customer buying it is the life or death of their business. Better to know before you go if you've got an idea that the marketplace will buy.

If you're radically changing fields, however, and starting up your company from scratch, it may be more difficult for you to get your first customer before you leave. Our recommendation is to do whatever it takes to test out your idea on as many prospects as possible and work to sign up your first customer. This kind of determination is the key to your success in the future.

10. Get Emotionally, Financially, and Technologically Fit Before You Go

No matter what happens with your entrepreneurial idea, to take full advantage of future opportunities it is important to be as emotionally, financially, and technologically fit as possible. When it comes to successful entrepreneurs, fortune favors the fit. Three key areas to address immediately are:

- Get your family to buy in to your plan. Their emotional support is essential to your success.
- Pay off all debts possible. Borrow as much money as you can right now and put the money in a safe place. You might need every penny, and even if you don't you'll have a psychological edge, particularly when you're starting out.
- Get technologically smart. Learn what you can while you are still employed. Take every course you can on your company's time. Knowing how to be computer-smart could be the lifeblood of your new business, and when you're out on your own you won't have the time to take any courses. Improve your typing skills. Learn the basic word processing, spreadsheet, and accounting software programs. Peter C. Jones, a partner in his own publishing business, says that he finds the software program Quicken to be an invaluable business ally, helping him pay his bills and keep track of his money on a daily basis. When he knows he has a bill to be paid, he uses Quicken to make out the check, even if it's not due for months. Then he deducts this sum from his bank balance on Quicken. He doesn't actually send out the checks until the normal paying period, but this process gives him an accurate picture of how much he has to bring in to break even, and helps him resist the temptation of spending more than he should. Knowing the ins and outs of a computerized accounting system before you leave your job will really help you get your business started.

11. Don't Be Fed Up, Get Fired Up!

You are embarking on a great adventure to a destination that you have dreamed about. Enjoy it!

Services Available

Michael Gill and Sheila Paterson speak to conventions and organizations all over the world. They also have their messages available on audio and video tape.

In addition, Michael Gill and Sheila Paterson conduct seminars and in-depth consulting for large international companies, government agencies, and growing entrepreneurial ventures using a unique process called Entrepreneurial Marketing. Entrepreneurial Marketing is a proven strategic and creative discipline that offers a fast, focused, and futuristic approach to solving your toughest marketing problems.

For further information call

**Sheila Paterson and Michael Gill at (212) 888-4141.
Fax: (212) 334-4223.**